NOT MY FOOTSTEPS

◆

THE LONG JOURNEY OUT

Bryan Dean

iUniverse, Inc.
New York Lincoln Shanghai

NOT MY FATHER'S FOOTSTEPS
THE LONG JOURNEY OUT

Copyright © 2005 by Bryan Dean

All rights reserved. No part of this book may be used or reproduced by any means, graphic, electronic, or mechanical, including photocopying, recording, taping or by any information storage retrieval system without the written permission of the publisher except in the case of brief quotations embodied in critical articles and reviews.

iUniverse books may be ordered through booksellers or by contacting:

iUniverse
2021 Pine Lake Road, Suite 100
Lincoln, NE 68512
www.iuniverse.com
1-800-Authors (1-800-288-4677)

ISBN: 0-595-33786-4

Printed in the United States of America

I am grateful in the writing of this my first book, to many different people. My wife supported me according to our wedding vows taken thirty-eight years ago, in sickness and in health. I have always known that she was my best friend. The trials which I put her through were traumatic, yet she stood beside me as I worked through this trying period. I will always love you!

My friend, 'Jack' was always there for me since our first acquaintance. Any time of day I could count on him for guidance and understanding. God sent him to me when He knew I needed a true friend in whom I could confide my deepest concerns. He facilitated my spiritual awakening. He set me on this path with patience and love.

Two counselors guided me along the way and helped me to understand where I was coming from, where I was currently in my life and who I really was.

Mike was the first man to whom I ever felt comfortable in revealing my darkest secrets. He literally held my hand and encouraged me to open the doors which had been closed all my life. He enabled me to remove my 'masks'.

'Lori' was my spiritual counselor. In some uncanny way, her Sunday talks were always directed to me personally. God's words, as spoken by her, gave me the strength and courage to BE and let Spirit guide me. After almost forty years I was spiritually awakened. In her presence every Sunday I was moved along in my quest for peace and joy. She opened my second door. Bless you 'Lori'…I miss you…

Finally, I want to acknowledge Chris. He was the real key in this journey. Without his online friendship, albeit brief, I might never have been able to make this journey. With the patience and understanding of a much older man than he really was, he helped me open that first door! We underwent many trials which are fully explained as you read this story. I have no regrets whatsoever about our relationship. I know God will be good to him for the rest of his life. He was there for me. God will be there for him as he struggles to find the happiness which he justly deserves. To Chris' friend, Michael…I forgive!

Pollo…I love you!

November 24, 2004

And so I had come to this point in my life, never having known pure joy.

No event or occasion could be recalled that evoked such exhilaration. For fifty years I had cocooned myself from such feelings, fearful that such intense emotion would, at most, be fleeting and ultimately replaced by great throes of anxiety.

My life was not meant to be joyous, as for some unknown reason, God required me to go through life penitent. On a thousand occasions, I had envisioned putting a gun to my temple, hoping to ease the self-inflicted agonies, the triumvirate of anxiety, loneliness and foreboding. But for want of a real gun, which I knew full well was not likely to be gotten in Canada; the trigger remained cocked in my mind. I knew that there was only one way out of life, but the road seemed endless.

God must have a plan, but what? But when? Would it ever be divulged to me?

As I looked into the eyes of my newborn grand-daughter, my second, my mind wandered to my own travails of life.
I was born in a small rural community. My father, a farmer, had married my mother when both were nineteen years old. They lived right next door to my paternal grandparents on the family farm. A sister, born four years earlier, completed my family. Just down the road lived my uncles and a variety of cousins creating what would come to be known as a nuclear family, before it became fashionable.

On my paternal side were a dozen siblings, the result of my grandmother's first and second marriages.
My mother had been raised by her paternal grandparents after her parents were separated shortly after her birth. For some time, the only thing I knew about my grandfather was that he was a circus worker, making candy floss in small towns across the country. Until later in life, sometime in early adolescence, I had no real knowledge of my maternal grandmother.

Two incidents remained frozen in my mind concerning my paternal grandfather, James—painting his Model A and seeing him dead in his favourite rocking chair, the actual circumstances washed from my memory. Curious memories…the memory of the faces forever erased. Of my paternal grandmother, Edna, the memories were slightly more expansive. She moved into a self-contained apartment in the family homestead after her husband's death. Somewhat later, she was taken on a Christmas vacation to Florida by her son, my father, leaving his wife and two children behind.

It was my maternal great grandfather who proved to be the constant through my early years. In fact, one of my earliest memories was of traveling by bus to the city where he bought me a suit, no doubt, so we could attend church together on Sunday, as grandpa was extremely religious, having been brought up in the Salvation Army. It was not unusual for grandpa to bicycle the seven miles from his home in town to our home in the country. He was the one who bought me my first two-wheeler—a second-hand one which I had had painted a bright yellow…strange color for a boy's bicycle? The bike provided me my first real taste of independence; the freedom to go anywhere the wheel would carry me.

The seasons of my childhood reflected my rural roots. Springtime on the farm equated with birth. Newborn farm animals, budding fruit trees, tulips groping for the sunshine, grass turning green after a long, dreary winter. Springtime was the promise—the promise of future joy which I would find perpetually illusive. Springtime was a sensual assault on my being. Robins, blue jays and cardinals filled my ears with their joyous cries, my eyes with their colorful plumage. The many spring flowers competed for my visual and aural attention. Pussy willows swayed in the wind, waiting patiently for my touch, much like the newborn calves who eagerly awaited my scratching of their heads and rubbing of their backs.

Like all farmers, my father was overwhelmed with work in the springtime. In addition to the regular chores, tending and milking cattle, it was time to ready the farm machinery for the season's work ahead. The kingpin of the farm was the large, green John Deere tractor, one of many that would make the farm its home over the years. It dwarfed all the other farmer's tractors in the area, and looking back, I realized it was a true status symbol, a sign of my father's success as a farmer. He could afford the biggest and best equipment!

The same was true of the cattle—all Holsteins, those black and white milk wagons. Every morning and again at night they would be 'emptied'—the old-fashioned way, although later on my father would be one of the pioneers, utilizing electric milking machines.

When he wasn't cleaning machinery, or milking cows, my father's attention was to crops to be planted, fields to be prepared for corn and tomatoes and wheat and oats. Little wonder he had so little time for his children or his wife.

Besides the farm labor, my father had other interests. For as long as I could remember my father had been a volunteer fireman and a school bus driver. The fire hall was a mile from the farm. It housed the large red fire truck that raced to fires throughout the township and occasionally into the nearby town when there was a really big fire. Every Monday night would be spent at the fire hall, cleaning equipment and hoses. While the firemen attended to this, my mother, sister and I would join the fire chief's wife for an evening of television and popcorn. Television in the fifties consisted of westerns and comedy shows. Two of the most popular shows were Gabby Hayes, a western, and I Love Lucy, the latter a Monday night institution, both viewed in black and white.

Bus driving was a weekly routine. Every morning my father pulled the big yellow bus out of the barn, boarded his two children and headed out on his route. Every evening the route was reversed. My sister and I were the first ones on the bus and the last ones off ever night, after cleaning the bus of debris. This was all of our elementary school lives.

School, of course, was the primary social and educational vehicle of my young life. It was the source of learning and of friendships outside my extended family of nearby cousins.

Occasionally, Saturday nights would find my family at the local town hall where my father indulged his hobby as a drummer in a three piece band. This was likely where the roots of his son's musical interests were nurtured.

Springtime on the farm was a time of discovery and exploration. Rains filled the enormous roadside ditches, Manmade floating devices allowed us to sail the 'rivers'. When the waters subsided, we would go hunting muskrats, exploring the ever present muskrat holes; half-hoping that none would come out, as their ferocity was well known. When we tired of this activity, we became dam builders, young engineers experimenting with altering the flow of the waters. When the waters were all gone, coincidentally so was springtime. The hope of spring became the reality of summer. The reality was announced by the end of the school year in June. Summer was supposed to be a kid's favourite season.

The seeds of the fall harvest had been planted. As the crops began to spring from the ground, the tomato plants had been installed in their rows, later to be picked by the hired workers from the city. Summer meant work and play for us on the farm. No more building dams or sailing boats. There was work to be done, the type of work able to be done by pre-teen boys, consisting primarily of spending eight hours a day hoeing weeds from between the rows of corn and tomatoes, of which there were over one hun-

dred acres on our farm. Beyond that were the same duties on the farms of my boyhood friends. Many of my friends also happened to be my cousins, some younger, some older. Such was my circle of friends.

Summer was never a time for family vacations, nor was any other season for that matter. After completing our farm chores, we would hop on our bikes and travel throughout the community. In our pre-teen years, the traveling took us to each other's houses and farms, and gradually the corner store, which was also the hub of the community. It was truly a community centre for the rural community. As it so happened, it was situated right beside the fire hall. Part general store, soda bar, gas station and pool hall, it was the epicenter of the rural universe, operated by a character named 'Digger' who was more of a grandfather than many of our own.

In return for help stocking shelves, sweeping up and pumping gas, the neighborhood boys received free pop, chocolate bars and ice cream. It seemed a perfect arrangement. As we became older, payment also included free use of the pool tables. With little other amusements available, this became our favourite hangout. Much of the summer was spent there or riding our bikes around the countryside, including the nearby beach.

Mine was not a religious family. My father's parents were Roman Catholic. My mother belonged to the United Church. I did not realize the importance of this difference until much later in life. Sundays were not spent in church, but on baseball diamonds where my father played amateur baseball in a county league. Every Sunday in the summer would see our family traveling to a different town's diamond, playing a different team. While the fathers played ball, the mothers would watch and gossip. The kids would be off, drinking pop and otherwise goofing off. Games seemed to last forever, well beyond the usual nine innings, after which were the familiar beer parties, where women would watch and gossip while their spouses overindulged in tubs of cold beer. This became a ritual of summer, albeit not one of my favourites. I would be an adult before I would bring myself to drink beer. Memories of summers long passed would prevent me from overindulging in the frothy, cold, brown liquid.

Throughout the spring and summer of my childhood, my mother, and for that matter, my sister played insignificant roles. Farm society was primarily a male dominated one. Farm wives had a role to play, but it was a traditional one—child rearing and housekeeping. Everything the women did would revolve around their husbands. No doubt this resulted in my viewing my mother's presence and importance of a lesser significance. She periodically ventured out with other farm wives to play cards—euchre or canasta. Shopping monthly for groceries in the city was infrequently accompanied with shopping for clothing for her or the children. Mondays were wash *days. In the summer or late fall she might do some canning. If equipment broke down on the farm, she would be summoned to go for parts.*

She was also the parental liaison with the school. While my father drove the school bus, he rarely was seen in the school. Every winter would see my mother helping out in the school kitchen, providing hot soup for the school children. She belonged to the Home and School Association. She encouraged my interest in vocal music, chauffeuring me to weekly vocal and piano classes and the many music festivals where I competed as a child. I actually won several vocal competitions. The trophies and plaques could be seen on display at the school. Although nothing was ever said, looking back, I believed my father never really approved of my interests. I tried to please him by joining baseball leagues in spring and summer, and occasionally putting on skates in the winter, but I never really excelled at either, and the interest waned before high school.

Summer ended in 1956!

It culminated with a trip to a movie theatre in the city, just father and children. Ironically the movie was "Tammy and the Bachelor". This was to be the last outing involving father and son!

Shortly thereafter, my father packed his clothes and left the farm, heading to the home of his brother, my uncle, in a small town one hundred and fifty miles away. Left behind was the farm, the fire hall, the baseball diamonds, the community centre, the school bus...his wife and two children....

Children never want to believe the evidence behind such behaviour—the overheard arguments which both my sister and I were aware of, my mother's accusations of Dad having an affair with our twenty-three year old babysitter, the trips alone to Florida with my grandmother. All of these contributed to the initial separation.

As often happens, daughters side with their fathers; sons, especially minor ones, side with mothers. Communication breakdown. In the process of choosing with whom to live, my sister was to choose my father. Would she ever come to realize much later the error of her choice, one which would leave an indelible mark on her life forever?

I was not given a choice! I was a minor and would be expected to stay with my mother in the family home. I was much too young to be concerned about how we would survive without a breadwinner...

My mother was fortunate to land a job at a local amusement park for the summer. Her grandfather worked there and was able to get her 'in'. How she got to and from work has long since been forgotten. Dad took the car. Her job in the dining room provided much needed food—leftovers from the kitchen at night—turkey, roast beef, mashed potatoes and sometimes pie.

When the season ended she was once again unemployed. There was no such ting as Unemployment Insurance back then. She had no real education or skills to get another job right away. With school starting, clothes were needed for me (and herself for that matter). By this time she had begun to see 'someone'—one of the many men who would come in and out of my life through my teenage years. They were all nice men, I guess. My father was providing fifteen dollars a month for my upkeep. Hardly adequate for a teenage boy. Money was needed for food, utilities, clothing and transportation, as well as the recently acquired divorce lawyers. My great grandfather provided whenever he could. I really don't know how we survived...

One day in September 1956, I was headed home on the school bus when I observed an ambulance in front of our house. I got off the bus and ran to see what I had never expected at my young age. My mother, in a state of desperation, had attempted suicide with an overdose of her 'nerve' pills, as they were called back then. Fortunately, she had called for help prior to passing out. She barely survived, but was not hospitalized. What would follow would be hours of psychiatric appointments to help her overcome this despair. This incident would become a defining moment in my lifetime of insecurity and anxiety; I knew I would have to take charge of my own situation. I was the key to my mother's recovery. But I was only a boy!

Our first Christmas alone was celebrated with turkey and presents. The former came in a Goodwill basket with other necessities. The later were acquired by my maternal great grandfather and through my mother's volunteer work with Toys for Tots type organization. I especially liked the full sized bow and arrow set I received. Strange—looking back I can NEVER remember receiving any gift from my paternal grandparents ever!

The winter snows made our lives seem bleaker. Heavy snows regularly blocked the roads and closed the schools. Our home, although heated by an oil stove, was old and drafty. Bales of straw formed a wall around the foundation. Water pipes were often frozen. Electricity often failed in the ice storms. We persevered, somehow. Neighbors offered rides into town for the few groceries we could afford. I had numerous cousins living on the Concession who continued to include me in their daily activities. My closest friend's father a second cousin) would take on the role my own father had never *assumed*—mentor and role model. *A man of modest means and education, he nevertheless tried tirelessly to include me as often as was possible in his own family's activities. When he could, he would pay me small amounts of money for helping on his farm. He taught me how to drive a tractor and operate various farm machinery. At mealtime, I was often included whether it was breakfast, lunch or dinner.*

This was especially beneficial, when, in the spring, my mother got a job as a cashier in a local grocery store. Her hours of work meant she was often away at lunch, and often late for dinner. Stores in those days only stayed open until six o'clock and Fridays until nine o'clock. With a steady income now, she was finally able to raise up her head. Shortly thereafter, we would leave the family farm house and move to another house a few miles away—away from my friends and cousins…

Divorce was very uncommon back then. There was a certain stigma attached to it. Further, my father was Roman Catholic. The Church did not condone it. The only legal grounds for divorce were for adultery. I didn't know what that meant for a long time. It turned out that my father's affair with the babysitter was just that. But by this time, my father had moved on—both to another town and woman. More lawyers…more private detectives…more money to pay them, both! It eventually was finalized; I can't exactly remember when.

In a real sense, I grew up without father or mother. While my father had made a choice, my mother's absence in my life was not her fault, she became the breadwinner. With no extra money from my father, she fended as best she could. We divided the household responsibilities. Mother worked to buy groceries, clothing and pay the bills. Charge cards were non-existent. If you had no money, that was too bad. My job was to go to school during the day. After school I would cook and clean house. On weekends mother did the laundry. Life was simple. I wanted pop or candy—I took empty pop bottles to the store and got a refund—two cents per bottle! I was alone most of the time. My reliance on my peers, especially one particular cousin, was not unexpected. Slightly older by five months, and seemingly more worldly, he became my peer teacher in so many ways.

My cousin had a knack for getting into minor troubles at home, over which his mother had little control. Living in their house was his paternal grandmother, who also had little control of him. This set the stage for many misadventures. We bicycled everywhere. Over the next few years we would be inseparable—almost brothers.

THE MARRIAGE

As I watched her walk down the aisle of the small Anglican Church, her father beside her, I wondered what the future would hold for us.

We had met in high school; she lived in a nearby town. The high school served a wide region. All of my cousins and friends were there too. My older sister had gone there before moving away with my father. I was introduced to 'her' through one of my classmates, who shared the same first name as her. At first we just hung out at lunch and after school, while waiting for our respective school buses. We were all friends. After school we would talk on the telephone (no Internet then—for that matter, no computers) about anything and everything. She was my first real girlfriend; we went to the school proms together, shopping in the city and to occasional movies. Sometimes I went to her house for dinner and sometimes she went with me to my great grandparents for Sunday dinner. We were reliant on our parents for transportation, as, at first neither had a driver's license. This somewhat complicated our relationship, but it worked at the time.

We weren't always in the same classes, so we shared stories of our daily activities. Summers were different—we lived so far apart, She had a part-time job by then. To compensate I would hang out with other boys around the farm when we didn't have chores to do. I spent hours at my cousin's farm involved in various farm activities and other activities—smoking chestnut pipes, building tunnels in the bales of straw in the barns, etc. Like most adolescent boys reaching puberty (or so I thought then) we experimented with tobacco and alcohol, the former smuggled out of my cousin's fathers packages, the latter from the open liquor cabinets. We advanced to real cigarettes 'purchased' from the corner store where we worked. Cancer was never a concern, not having been linked to smoking in the fifties.

Looking back, I was never able to pinpoint when, where or how our sexual experimentation began. All of my cousins were older and puberty had already begun. Somewhere I learned about erections and masturbation, wet dreams and sex in general and it certainly wasn't at school back then. They say peer education is the primary source for young males and that must have been the case for me. Every once in awhile, the guys would get together at someone's house and see who could masturbate first. There was no touching, but lots of opportunity to observe other guys' genitals. We never once thought we were gay, a term which was not even in the sexual vocabulary of the fifties. It was all so normal growing up. We weren't QUEER!

There was no overt sexual activity with my future wife, beyond kissing when no one was looking. We'd hold hands, but common to the times, any real sexual activity was put off before marriage. We dated throughout the early high school years. In the summer following grade eleven, my mother took a job in a city 100 miles away.

I always believed the move was a desperate attempt to reunite with my sister who now was living only thirty minutes from our new place.

Although only four years older, she had left home at sixteen to live with our father. While living with him she met her future husband and became engaged. She came home to get married shortly thereafter, already pregnant with her first child! She immediately returned to her father's new town, moving in with her new husband's family.

At first the move to a big city was exciting, but it soon became very lonesome. No longer able to talk on the telephone for long hours, I was relegated to listening to records (no CD's back then), doing homework and window shopping in the big department store downtown, for things I couldn't afford to buy. I had no friends there. Everything we owned was secondhand, including the bunk beds, separated, which we slept on in the single bedroom of the basement apartment. While mother worked at the nearby grocery store, I attended school. After school, I'd be home alone, listening to music and preparing supper for the two of us. Meals were never eaten out. Too costly. Ours was a humdrum life of routine. No frills. After one year mother accepted a transfer back to my old community when a new store opened. I stayed on to finish school (barely) sell off our possessions, load up the family car (after using money from the furniture sale for car repairs) and drive home alone once again.

Initially we lived with friends; I slept on a couch. Eventually we found a one-bedroom apartment in the upstairs of a house nearby. I had graduated from high school and applied to Teachers' College. When my application was delayed due to relocating, I went back for a fifth year of high school. I stayed one week; I was accepted to College. Once there I found myself with familiar faces—my girlfriend, along with a number of former high school friends.

THE CAREER

Teaching had not been my first choice as a career. In high school I had considered physiotherapy—even spent a few days visiting hospitals. The bottom line—there was no money for schooling. Teachers' College was free at that time and a university degree was not required. As a youngster I remembered my family doctor telling me he started as a teacher until he could afford money for medical school. The concept stuck with me, and in September 1963 I became a student teacher at eighteen years of age! At that time male students wore suits and ties. That was the way teachers dressed back then, with little extra money, my mother found some used suits and sport coats and I was dressed to go.

Teachers' College was not a challenge. I had been a very good student in high school until transferring to the other city. What made it bearable were the stints of 'practice teaching' in real schools, something that occurred many times throughout the year. I soon came to realize that I was good at this and began to enjoy it.

During my first practice teaching week in a grade six class, I along with millions of others around the world, experienced the assassination of United States President John Fitzgerald Kennedy in Dallas, Texas on November 22, 1963. The exact moment of hearing the news would be forever etched in my memory. November 22nd would take on a different significance forty years later!

At the end of the first year, I was at the College when I received a phone message from my mother—my father had died of an apparent heart attack. He was only forty-two years old. I didn't realize at the time, but would later come to understand the full impact of his death.

At the time of the funeral I was devoid of emotion. I can't remember crying. After all, this was the father who had deserted me seven years earlier, when he ran off with the babysitter. As a token, my paternal uncles gave me my father's signet ring, which, ironically my mother had given him several years earlier. It seemed a hollow gesture. It made my uncles feel better, I guessed. In fact it was much too big for me to wear, as even then I had small, unmanly hands and fingers.

When summer arrived that year I was relieved. No more school. No more concerns about my absentee father. I had my whole life ahead of me…

Summer was completely leisure. Unlike my girlfriend, I had no real job. I passed my time visiting her at work at a local department store and talking on the telephone. No job meant no money. For entertainment, we would sometimes go to the movies. Most of the time we sat at her parents' home watching television. Sometimes we visited her sister's home, eating pizza and drinking Mateus wine. On one occasion, after too much wine and too little pizza, I awoke the next morning with my future wife's grandmother looking in on me. "Poor guy—must be the flu!" For reasons which I had forever blotted out, we were to break up that summer.

In the fall, I returned to Teachers' College in my final year and threw myself into my studies and teaching assignments. As part of our studies, each graduating class was responsible for a literary production. Besides the work of a student teacher, a classmate and I volunteered to write the script for our production of **Animal Farm** *by George Orwell. The production included my entire class in a black light production where all of the cast members wore black clothing and full head masks representing the animals, and painted with a special paint that could only be seen when the black lights were on. It was a great success. I always knew I wrote well.*

As my college life was ending, my former girlfriend's girlfriend was getting married. We too had been friends throughout high school. In fact, it was she who had introduced us.

I attended the wedding in a neighbouring town church, where, of course, I once again was in the presence of my future wife. Things evolved and the relationship was rekindled.

We both were offered teaching contracts by the local school board, which we accepted enthusiastically. In September 1965, we started on the long road which would be our careers for life. She started as a primary teacher; I started as an elementary school science teacher. At Christmas, we became engaged. Eight months later we would be married. My bride was just twenty-one years old; I was nineteen, which meant my mother had to sign the marriage license. Our differences in age would be a lifelong source of harmless joking.

Thirty-two years later we would be retiring, culminating long careers with the same school board. Over the years we both changed schools several times. After eleven years I transferred to the secondary schools. During the course of my elementary school years I had taught all grades and all subjects. In my last few years in the elementary schools, I was a full-time teacher-librarian, a job that involved teaching students' research skills and instilling in them a love for reading and literature.

When I started teaching in the secondary schools, it was the first opportunity to make use of my university studies, which I had been pursuing nights and summer during my early teaching assignment. I had graduated from the local university with a degree in political science and communication studies (mass media) in 1972. My great grandfather attended the ceremony, beaming with pride. At the secondary school I was responsible for the school library and also taught the students about mass media, Canadian law and mathematics. In actuality, this was a vocational school, so keeping the students interest was always a challenge. I remained there for seven years before transferring to an academic secondary school.

In the course of my remaining years as a full-time teacher-librarian I would become president of the provincial school library association, a source of great personal satisfaction, marred only by the fact that the organization was 'metro centric' in its operations and procedures. I was an outsider who attempted to challenge the status quo—a challenge which I soon realized would be futile. Nevertheless, as a member of the organization, I would be deeply involved in their major conferences, organizing all aspects of the conferences with other association members—another source of professional pride. In the course of our teaching careers, we had raised two daughters. Our oldest was born in our third year of marriage. At that time, a woman was required to resign from teaching. Maternity or paternity leaves were unheard of.

THE FAMILY

Our first daughter was a healthy, sensitive, energetic and beautiful baby. She was always eager to please her parents and grandparents. When she was about six years old, she was joined by a sister—another healthy and beautiful baby. Life was great. We had our own home, two lovely kids and good jobs. We also had many friends—almost all were teachers…All of them were young and eager. We shared life's moments—weddings, births and occasionally deaths. Our friends were mostly my wife's girlfriends and their husbands.

As a family, we vacationed together on a regular basis. I wasn't about to repeat my father's actions…leaving his family behind while he vacationed with his mother! Our first big vacation was by airplane to Hawaii (the first time any of us had flown). The girls remember it because in almost all of the photographs they were dressed in matching muumuus which their mother had made for them for the trip. It was Christmas. Santa came on the airplane! Subsequent trips would include Florida, the Bahamas, the east coast of Canada, Quebec and the American Southwest, specifically Arizona and California.

The girls often spent time with their maternal grandparents, allowing their parents some free time. Rarely, the paternal grandmother and her spouse of the time would take care of them—usually limited to a few hours. More than likely for these reasons, the girls never had a close relationship with my mother. She never really knew how to be a grandmother, probably due to the fact that she herself had been raised by an autocratic grandmother, the first wife of my beloved great grandfather, the same who gave me my first bicycle.

School years were always somewhat complicated for the girls with parents as teachers. Other teachers had expectations of teachers' children. Parents who were teachers knew what type of education their children should be receiving. Both girls did fairly well in school, although the younger daughter would constantly be compared to her sister. Throughout most of their school lives both girls excelled. They had many friends.

Everything changed for the younger one when—when she was in grade seven, their beloved maternal aunt suddenly died of a stroke at forty years of age. It was Christmas of 1985; they experienced death first hand, at a time when both were old enough to comprehend the devastation. Life changed for their family from that day on…

My wife's youngest sister was a little over a year younger. Theirs had been a challenged family economically. Both parents worked hard to support their five children—two boys and three girls. A third brother died in infancy. Not until their teenage years did their parents buy a house, having always lived in rental accommodation. In actuality there were two families; the oldest brother was over ten years older than the youngest sister. In the younger girl's teen years they alone shared the family home with their parents. The oldest brother had joined the Air Force and moved on. The oldest sister married at eighteen and left the home. The so-called middle child, their brother was briefly at home during the girls early teenage years, but left when he began working for a bank—to which he would rise to vice-president before retirement. The youngest sister was certainly the most challenging for her parents. She also married young, actually before her sister, and divorced after half a dozen years, becoming a single mother to her young son. She too had been attracted to banking, a career which would take her far away to Toronto and a very good job with the same bank. While there she met and eventually married her second husband, also a banker, who had come to Canada from England a few years earlier. Her son would eventually leave to live with his biological father, while his mother and her new husband would adopt a baby girl. The baby was a little over two years old when her mother died decorating the Christmas tree in their new home. She had an aneurism.

The call had come in the middle of the night. Our distraught brother-in-law would only say that his wife was in the hospital unconscious from a probable stroke. Our family quickly packed the family car and collected her son from his father's home. The long drive took four hours, four hours spent in total silence as the five of us relived our moments with mother, sister and aunt. When we arrived at the hospital we were told that she was brain dead, but breathing as a result of mechanical means. The decision was made to allow her to die in dignity after harvesting vital body organs for eventual transplant. We said our goodbyes and left the hospital to prepare for her funeral.

No one could have predicted the fallout from her untimely death. Of course it deeply affected all family members, but at that time, the repercussions to my own young daughter were almost instantaneous.

Her interest in school declined. She suffered a major attitude adjustment and began hanging out with all the wrong people. As she progressed from grade school to high school, her disposition did not improve. The school was forever calling about her attendance, or lack of it. This once bright young girl was in a downward spiral. Her *choices of friends got worse. She became deceptive and stayed out late, becoming a major threat to our marriage. We joked that the first one to leave the house had to take the kids, but seriously, at that time, our lives were on a roller coaster—the ups and downs of dealing with a rebellious teenager.*

Meanwhile, our oldest daughter completed high school and entered university. Life with her sister was difficult to say the least. She worked part-time at various jobs and ended her university years working at a bank, just like her aunt. She eventually found a job in the offices of a national automotive manufacturer, found a steady boyfriend and moved to Toronto, where she lived for about a year in her own apartment, before returning home once again. Shortly after, her younger sister moved out to live with her own boyfriend. He would be one of the many bad decisions she would make over the next few years.

THE GRANDPARENTS

Several years and several boyfriends later, our youngest daughter would find herself pregnant with her first child. We would soon become grandparents. Marriage was not an option for her. The father of her unborn child was usually unemployed, scrambling for various sources of income and always short of the prize.

Life with him was difficult—a small apartment in an old house with very little material wealth and very little emotional health. Were it not for our daughter finding a regular job, the family would have been homeless. With our support, groceries were on the table, rent arrears paid and our newborn granddaughter clothed and fed. Her mother was a very kind and loving parent, albeit unprepared for motherhood. The same could not be said for the baby girl's father. We would eventually learn that he had already fathered a son by another woman years before he met our daughter.

Their lives were not easy—neither for parents or child. The young couple struggled from day one. He found work and then lost it as quickly. Various income making schemes fell through. He had left home around sixteen years of age—no longer abiding by his parents' rules. Finishing school was not an option he ever fully considered. His was a life spent in various friends' houses sharing accommodations until the friends caught on to his devious ways. His newborn daughter would live in four or five different apartments in the first years of her young life. Screaming, fighting and cockroaches were with her wherever they lived. Each time the couple moved, we would be there helping, cleaning, painting, packing…whatever support we could offer.

Finally the young family moved into an apartment not far from us. While it was a large place and moderately clean, it didn't change the dynamics of the relationship. They bickered about life, his inability to find work, how to pay their bills each month and even about raising their daughter.

All of this stress and strain came to an end one summer evening when our daughter arrived home after being with her girlfriend, to find another woman in her bed! The resultant shouting and screaming ended with the police being summoned. Our daughter's girlfriend had the sense to call us. Off to the rescue I went. After that mother and daughter returned to our home. We thought he was out of the picture and could be assured that our daughter and her daughter were safe again. Once again there were now four people living in our home.

We tried very hard not to interfere in our daughters' upbringing of her daughter. We encouraged the paternal grandparents to be involved in her life, though we discouraged her father. Rarely did we talk about him in front of his daughter. We were extremely relieved when he moved three hours away thus lessening his influence on his baby daughter. We encouraged our daughter to seek a legal separation or divorce (even though theirs was a common law marriage), something she was reticent to do because he had threatened a custody battle. She knew he would never win, but she couldn't and wouldn't take the chance of losing her only child. He was a man with a terrible temper, of which she was well aware, having been the brunt of it on many occasions.

During this period our eldest daughter met a young man while working in the bank. She had been introduced by a co-worker. Unlike her sister's "spouse" this young man was highly responsible and confident, coming from a very solid home where he had been the youngest of three sons. With her younger sister back home, our oldest daughter saw an opportunity to move out once again—this time with her boyfriend.

Neither we nor his parents made an effort to stop the arrangement. She was old enough to know what she wanted. The young couple were both university graduates; both were employed and very mature. They moved in together with our blessing and eventually became engaged in a whirlwind trip to New York. He proposed while ice skating at Rockefeller Center.

By this time, our younger daughter had become involved with another man—this time one that was responsible and gainfully employed in a trade. After a short period they moved in together, with him dutifully taking on the role of father to her child. Theirs was not a stress free relationship. They lived together for several months as a family, until one night he came home from work to find she had gone off with one of his male friends. He abruptly left, devastated by her dishonesty.

In spite of his hurt, he was a forgiving man. They would be apart for a short while before they reconciled and found a new home of their own in a geared-to-income townhouse. It was there where they would decide to expand their family, resulting in the birth of another daughter, four years younger than her sister.

RETIREMENT YEARS

By this time we had both retired from our teaching careers. My wife was now employed part-time in a clothing store in a mall. I started work in a big box building materials store. In January 1999 our oldest daughter was married. She and her husband purchased a home in a suburb of the city. Theirs was far from a traditional relationship. After becoming engaged her husband to be set off on a four month trip to Southeast Asia to fulfill a dream of a lifetime. Our daughter joined him for a few weeks before he left for Vietnam. While there, he had ordered the wedding invitations, putting into gear their wedding plans. They chose January 9, 1999 as their wedding date—1-9-99 (1999) a cold day to say the least with a heavy snow the evening before. Following the wedding they set sail on a honeymoon cruise to the Caribbean.

Life was good for us. We were both retired and now had found meaningful part-time work, which I claimed was mental health insurance—something to keep us both busy. (Looking back I wondered about the truth of that statement). We were doting grandparents to our two granddaughters. Our lives revolved around the two little girls. Our work schedules took into account our oldest granddaughter's school hours, so we would be there whenever needed, morning, noon or night. Two girls became three when our oldest daughter gave birth in 2001 to her first child. Three months after her birth, her parents and the two of us set sail on a Caribbean cruise celebrating the marriage of her husband's best friends. It became a honeymoon cruise for all of the couples in the party, stopping at ports in San Juan, Aruba, Curacao, Saint Marten's and St. Thomas.

Two months after the cruise we were off for our annual trip to the Florida Panhandle, a place where we had begun vacationing following our retirements.
Life in Florida was pleasant—no snow to shovel, spring like weather and no children or grandchildren for whom to care. While 'grandma' thoroughly enjoyed our annual trip, I constantly agonized over my granddaughters' well being thousands of miles away in Canada. A single phone call could result in depression if there was a problem back home. Although I enjoyed being away with my wife, I couldn't take my mind off the grandchildren.

All my life I made mountains out of molehills. I had internalized my anxieties—about my family, my job and my life. With no male friends there was no one to whom I could unload my feelings. I was a man; men don't display emotion or share anxieties and insecurities. Men are supposed to be strong and emotionless.

The façade was soon to crumble—my world would come collapsing down on me sooner than expected!

THE ENDING

As we walked in the door of my house, I noticed that there was a telephone message. In the excitement of the moment I decided to ignore it, probably a telemarketer!

I accompanied the other man to the guest bedroom where we quickly undressed and began to explore each other's bodies. This ultimately led to mutual oral gratification, followed by the afterglow of just holding each other and tenderly caressing each other's bodies. It was all that I had anticipated it to be and none of what I thought it would be. What had begun in adolescence was buried throughout my marriage of thirty-seven years.

We had met on an adult chat line a few days earlier. With similar backgrounds (teachers) and similar playful needs we had arranged to meet at a local coffee shop before committing to the 'date'.

Fate intervened when, as we were culminating our encounter, I heard the familiar sound of the front door handle being turned. Before I knew it, the door opened and in walked my wife, calling my name. I quickly pulled on my jeans and went to greet her. It was too late, as my friend's shoes were at the front door, his van parked out front. I met her query of "who's here?" with a terse, "Just a friend". As she turned and walked out the door I knew the moment of truth had finally arrived. I could no longer hide my attraction to other men. I had been caught, literally with my pants down!

The road to this day had been a long one. I had always been faithful to my wife. I had had no physical contact with other men since I was seventeen years of age. When the urges overtook me, I would sometimes purchase gay magazines, which I would either quickly dispose of or hide in some crevice of our home, fearing all the time that either my wife or children would discover them.

I loved my wife, but I was also attracted to men. Summertime was great with so many men walking around in so little clothes, especially at the beach. For a brief time we had health club memberships. While we both went to workout in same sex gyms, I more enjoyed the after workout sessions where the naked men shared spas, saunas and showers. This made my blood pressure jump higher than the exercise. Sometimes my heart pounded so hard that I thought I'd have a heart attack. Headline—"Local teacher drops dead after vigorous exercise in gym." How surprised my colleagues would be if they knew it was not the exercise that killed me; it was the exercise of my lusting for men!

We purchased our first home computer several years before we had retired. Mostly early computers were used as word processors. Upon retirement we purchased a new computer. By this time, surfing the Internet was fairly common. While teaching, I had taken a short term sabbatical and written an Internet instruction manual for teachers.

One afternoon, while surfing the 'net for images of men, I discovered chat lines. This was not entirely new to me. My next door neighbour used chat lines to meet new friends. Cautiously, I attempted to 'log-in', not really knowing what to expect. My heart raced as I realized one such chat line allowed gay-oriented men to converse directly with one another—with complete anonymity. Within a few days, with my wife at work, I was chatting with the world. One of the 'cyberzens' was a twenty-three year old North Carolina university student. Little was I to know that the young man would forever impact the rest of my life!

LIFE WITH CHRIS

We had met on an adult chat line, primarily gay in nature. After we connected, we eventually moved to an immediate messaging (IM) service. At first these conversations were exchanges of weather, likes, dislikes, sports interests and the young man's academic life in North Carolina. As we got to know each other our conversations became more in-depth. Ultimately we started exchanging our deepest emotions and feelings, each sharing our fears and anxieties. Neither of us had ever been able to do this before.

About a month into our online friendship, my now closest friend dropped a bombshell—he was suffering from stomach cancer. He was taking large amounts of medication which sometimes made him cranky or sullen. There were no words which could possibly express the feelings upon learning of my friend's condition. I was shattered by the news.

Trying not to dwell on his illness, I directed the conversations away from the dreaded cancer, but it was always in the background like some overshadowing spirit. I could not, or did not want to realize the man's illness would be terminal. In the ensuing days, I would begin to talk more frankly to my friend, online and eventually by telephone. The calls were made discreetly using a phone card, thereby eliminating the fear of my wife's learning of the relationship. She was already suspicious of the late hours I would spend on the computer, when she was asleep.

Our first phone call was rather stilted—both of us felt nervous, finally hearing each other's voice. The call was all too short. Subsequent calls would last up to an hour, with discussions of a very serious, if not somewhat intimate nature. Having had no real male friends for almost forty years, the young man became the friend I'd never had, my only friend since adolescence.

One thousand miles apart, but it was like we had known each other forever. It became increasingly hard to end our conversations. Neither wanted to be the one to say goodnight. Eventually the "Goodnight" was followed by "Love you".

I began to contemplate a new and different life. We had discussions of getting together and traveling after he graduated from university. Life in North Carolina was not glamorous or exciting and just maybe that is what I represented to my friend, Chris.

Many nights a week I would put on my CD player and a favourite CD and go for long walks in the dark. During those times I contemplated both life and death, actually two lives—my present with all the normal trappings—family and work and the future. I considered what a second life would be like with Chris. The sacrifices would be great for both of us.

I began to despair and retreat unto myself. To my wife I seemed sullen and aloof, no longer interested in day to day activities. Eventually both family and friends saw this change. Seeking an outlet for my emotional being, I once again turned to the Internet. I wasn't sure whether I was looking for a father figure, who I had never had, or a real life surrogate for my new friend Chris. The ensuing search nearly resulted in my death and potentially impacted on the health of my own wife who had stood by me all these years. Dr. Jekyll would eventually become Mr. Hyde.

THE TRANSFORMATION

The transformation was inevitable. One evening on the chat line I met a man in his thirties. The conversation moved quickly to a sexual tone. I was intrigued but anxious. The man invited me to a local gay bath house. At first I resisted the offer. A few exchanges later, after days of soul searching, I agreed to meet while my wife was at work. On the day of the assigned meeting, I nervously prepared for the encounter. On my way to the bath house I stopped to purchase condoms, lubricants and antiseptic wipes, preparing for any eventuality, not sure what to expect.

Upon entering the bath house I paid thirty dollars and was given a room key and two towels. Walking through the halls I found my assigned room and entered, locking the door behind me. I surveyed the surroundings—a small room with aging carpet, a single bed against the wall, with what appeared to be fresh sheets. I quickly undressed, placing the condoms on the small bed table along with the wipes and lubricants. One towel I wrapped around my middle-aged torso, the other I carried to the assigned meeting room where gay porn movies were shown. My partner had not yet arrived and so I sat, mesmerized by the movie which showed three young men engaged in various sexual activities.

After a while I became bored and went to seek out the man whom I had messaged. Nowhere could he be found. In fact, there was only one other person there and he was in the smoking room watching television, definitely NOT my date.

I decided to make use of the saunas and steam room, anticipating my partner's arrival. I couldn't believe I would be stood up on my first date. After one and a half hours of saunaing and steaming, I decided to go back to my room and get dressed. As I entered my room I heard a key turn in the adjacent room. Could this be my chat friend?

Unlocking my door I stepped out to see a forty-ish, long-haired man. This couldn't be the guy. I cautiously asked if the man wanted company. It was too late to go back now. My sexual appetite needed fulfillment. The other man groped my genitals through the towel and invited me to the showers. Once in the showers, the groping became mutual. The towels hung on nearby hooks while each of us exposed ourselves to the eyes and hands of the other. Both of us were now highly stimulated. It was time to return to our room to continue satisfying our mutual desires.

During the encounter I became lost in my actions. After thirty-seven years, the desires I had experienced as a teenage boy returned. This was no fantasy! It was real. It was exciting. It was what I had been longing for, for such a long time. Here I was in bed with a totally naked man, giving and receiving mutual oral pleasures. I was certainly not attracted to this man. I knew that for sure. He was a vessel for my latent desires, now no longer latent…I did not experience orgasm. In fact, I had given the man a 'hand job', until he came, after which the stranger grabbed his towels and retreated to his own room.

I felt it had been a 'slam, bang, thank you mam' moment. After the stranger left, I lay there exposed and stroked myself to orgasm. Needless to say, my first real encounter had left me wanting—not wanting more, but unfulfilled by this liaison. I got dressed and left the bath house, vowing never to subject myself to such degradation again—at least for a couple of weeks.

There followed two other encounters with men, this time in our own home. One was an older man; the other was younger. Once again I was left unfulfilled. And so began my real quest…

FALL FROM GRACE

In mid-October 2003, on my fifty-eighth birthday I had a doctor's appointment. By this time, my fear, anxiety and guilt and shame were running rampant. My doctor had been treating me for mild depression for several months, not knowing the root of my feelings. After all, his patient was a middle-aged, well educated married man with children and grandchildren. He was successful in his chosen career. What was his problem?

In tears, I expressed a need for additional medication. Sensing a deepening crisis, the doctor asked me to complete a questionnaire, so as to gauge the depth of the depression. I didn't hold back. To the doctor's astonishment, this seemingly 'nice man' (the doctor's own words) was on the verge of suicide. Without hesitation I was directed to the local community crisis centre at a nearby hospital. I was interviewed by a young case worker, Jasmine.

My emotional floodgates burst, when for the first time in my life, at the exact age of fifty-eight years, I divulged to this total stranger, the roots and depths of my current state. Almost without hesitation, Jasmine knew I needed to see a psychiatrist. Cutting through the red tape of the emergency ward, she arranged a meeting. There was no doubt in her mind that I was a danger to myself and should be admitted without delay.

It was an agonizing time. I didn't come there to be admitted. I needed to talk. What would my wife and children think? What about my co-worker? I couldn't call my wife. I pleaded with the staff to let me go home and return the next day—hoping to explain to my wife why I was being admitted to the Psych Ward. They wouldn't be moved. Under authority of the Department of Health, I was to be admitted for no less than seventy-two hours, after which their decision would be revisited.

Sobbing uncontrollably, I asked Jasmine to contact my wife and then awaited her arrival, dreading the confrontation. I swore Jasmine and the psychiatrist NOT to divulge the real reason for my admission—confronting my apparent gayness or bisexuality. I still was not sure.

My wife arrived in tears, as expected about twenty minutes later. I explained to her that I was having trouble dealing with my past, especially my alienation from my father. My medications were inadequate. I was being admitted for further scrutiny, but I was being admitted to the Psych Ward—Intensive Care Unit. The staff was concerned about my state of mind.

She subsequently left the ER to tell the children at home. I laid back, now accepting my immediate fate. For now, I would be safe from myself and hopefully, as a result of Jasmine's intervention, I would once again be on the 'straight' track.

The first three days (72 hours) were eye openers. These patients were crazy! Although I had my own room, monitored by closed circuit camera, the door remained open day and night. The lights were left on. I was allowed no street clothes, no razor, no radios or CD—absolutely no objects which might cause me harm. My every move was monitored and recorded, including going to the bathroom. The first day I stayed in my room—waking, sleeping, waking, sleeping etc. I slept hoping to wake to find this was all a dream. I couldn't possibly be in this place. I wasn't crazy like the others who ranted and raved all night. So why was I under suicide watch? DAH…I had threatened such action in the doctor's office two hours earlier! [One week earlier, in desperation I had sat my wife down, face to face and explained that while I still loved her, I needed to either commit suicide or divorce her. It came out of the blue. We held each other with tears streaming down our faces that night.]

Hearing of my sexual escapades, the ward doctor asked me to submit to an HIV test. What had I done? What had I been thinking? How would my family react if it was positive? I couldn't sleep had it not been for the sedatives.

On day two I cautiously left my room to go to the TV room, where for a couple of hours I could try to take my mind off my status. I was allowed one visitor, once a day. The buzz of the intercom alerted the staff that a visitor had arrived. This was my wife, who, for the first time, now saw her husband as just one of the many crazed people in the ICU. I couldn't imagine what she was thinking. What had she told the children and her friends? Together we concocted a story of chemical imbalance, drug-induced. She knew this was not the case. I was having a mid-life crisis brought on by my previously stated paternal alienation. Lots of men undergo such crises. Now her husband of thirty-seven years was one such statistic. I wasn't about to tell her the truth. As I had told the caseworker…I would rather die than have my wife find out the truth.

That day I was moved to a room with a young man in his mid-twenties who was in severe depression as a result of a house fire in which his aunt and one child were engulfed in flames. Three children survived. He and his young wife had taken them in. He slowly deteriorated to the state he was in, trying to deal with his overwhelming grief.

On the fourth day of my stay, I was deemed well enough to be moved out of ICU. The new ward held about twenty patients. I knew now that I would soon be released.

After all, I was no longer suicidal. My wife and children could now visit. I was allowed to wear street clothes, use my razor, play my CD player, but could have no shoes, laces or belts. Every morning, noon and night I received my medications. I was still under close supervision, as were the other patients. Patients came and went on a regular basis, depending on the progression of their recovery.

My first roommate was an old, silent man suffering from Alzheimer's. He was sent to a nursing home. My second roommate was a male nymphomaniac. While having sex with two women, he had consumed too much alcohol along with barbiturates. Unable to arouse him(not in the sexual connotation) his companions called an ambulance and he was admitted to the Psych Ward.

Other patients included several drug addicts, mostly young men, an anorexic teenage girl, a teenage nymphomaniac(who tried to hit on the sleeping young men), a woman who drove her car into a tree in an attempt to commit suicide, a couple of obsessive compulsive types, a few people dealing with the stress of divorce, and a couple of alcoholics.

For the next nine days we would be family, along with the various doctors and nurses who treated us. Routine was the norm. Wake at seven o'clock, breakfast at seven-thirty. Meds at nine, smokes at nine thirty. From nine thirty to eleven we watched television, read, met with the support staff or psychiatrists, then once again gathered for lunch under the watchful eyes of our supervisors.

At some point during the day each patient met with their assigned nurse for evaluation on their progress. Two nurses in particular, one in ICU and one in the Step-Down Ward, proved to be my pseudo-psychiatrists.

It was the ICU nurse who first suggested I do some writing. Specifically she suggested that a good start would be writing a letter to my long deceased father in an attempt to explain my long pent up feelings of alienation. With trepidation I wrote (with a SAFE golf pencil) and cried—then wrote some more and cried until the letter was done.

Dear Dad

It's a beautiful day outside in October 2003 and here I am in the psychiatric ward at Hotel Dieu Hospital. I have been writing a journal of my life trying to figure out what has gone wrong with it. In so doing, I have just completed detailing my first eighteen years and you are almost a footnote! What more could you be? Unfortunately, you 'blew' that opportunity when you abandoned me and ran off with our babysitter, someone half your age. I have come to realize why you would have left Mom—she still isn't the easiest person to get along with and probably never was. I believe that two people shouldn't stay in a marriage for the sake of the children. But why did you divorce me? What did I do to deserve being left behind all those years? Being the only kid without a Dad? Was I too small? Did I have too many freckles? Was I not athletic enough? Did I look too much like my Mother that you couldn't look at me? I have never known the answer.

And if you really cared, why didn't you make more of an effort to see me? After all, your brothers lived right next door to us. You could have phoned, but then again Mom probably would have hung up on you. You had a car; we had to rely on friends to go anywhere.

Do you really appreciate how hard you made my young life? When other kids went out with their Dads, I was home alone because Mom had to go to work to support us. When other kids signed up for summer baseball I had no money for a glove or uniform. In the winter the other kids went skating with their new Christmas skates; I had to settle for second-hand. The only bicycle I ever had was a second hand one great grandpa gave me. All I can ever remember getting from you was a stuffed baby alligator and a shirt that was four sizes too big. Did you know I wore that shirt constantly until it wore out? You were a farmer, but you taught me very little about farming. You were a musician but you taught me nothing and never encouraged me to play an instrument. I had a very good singing voice and won many regional trophies but you were never there for any one of them and probably never knew.

In high school I was on the Honor Roll every year. I worked hard to get good marks, but you never saw any of them. I was a lousy shot in Cadet Corps and even worse in organized sports but I had a flair for writing (and I hope it shows here).

Through all of those years you were gone I had no male to whom I could ask the important questions—How do I tie a knot in a tie? How does one go about shaving? How can I do better in sports? What's hockey all about? Bet you didn't know I once had team photographs of all six original NHL teams? Seems such a long time ago...only six teams.

Mom worked hard to provide me with food and clothes, even if they were second hand. She bought food home from work so I was never hungry. Life was minimal—for snacks I had to collect pop bottles from the ditches by our house. If I was lucky I would get enough for a pop and some penny candy. I always looked to Halloween and all that free candy!

Did you ever remember my birthday was October 15th? I don't recall any cards EVER. Every year I waited but none came, nor did you call.

I will never forgive you for leaving your family at Christmas and taking your mother to Florida.

We moved to London in 1962—just one hour from you, but you never tried to contact me. I barely made it through high school after leaving all of my friends behind. Life was even tougher for us that year. We had a second hand car and furniture. We lived in a basement apartment where you could watch garter snakes being born in the spring…by the hundreds!

Did you ever think of driving over and taking me for an ice cream? Or a Sunday drive?

I started Teachers' College in 1963. Now back home, Mom spent seventy-five hard earned dollars to buy second hand suits so I'd be properly dressed. Where were you?

You never lived long enough to see me graduate and become a teacher. You missed my university graduation—the first in your family to do so. You left my life in June 1964 when you suddenly died. I can remember the phone call and then the thought—"Should I go to your funeral?"

I decided that I had to and Mom arranged for me to go. I can remember your coffin and the broken wheel of flowers which was also present when your brother died earlier…kind of a family tradition I guess. I remember your new wife, Irma, She seemed nice. I wish I could have known her better. Don't laugh—I do remember she made the best chicken curry I have ever tasted. I can never eat it without thinking of her to this day. The last thing I remember about your funeral was having your brothers give me your signet ring. I still have the stone and after this I am going to have it remounted and wear it. Maybe having a little piece of you with me will give me the strength I need to keep going.

I am really sorry you chose to miss my adolescence, even more that you missed my adult years. I graduated, started teaching, married a great girl, had two beautiful daughters and now have 3.5 grandchildren—three girls and a first grandson on the way…your great grandson!

Gloria and I retired in 1998 and now both have part-time jobs. Don't laugh at this one either…I am working in the paint department of a building supplies store. Remember when I painted your father's car?

Well that's about it. I have sorely missed you and visit your grave sometimes…for what I am not sure….

Be with me now!

Love
Your son

When my wife visited I allowed her to read the letter, hoping that this would shed some light on why I was here in the first place. She read it without questioning. I didn't think she really believed this tactic.

In the Step-Down ward my nurse was a previously married woman named Maureen. In the course of our daily briefings she had confided her marital history and unfaithful spouse whom she subsequently divorced. She was a "Dutch Aunt" if there was ever such a person. She gave it to me straight. Who did I think I was? What kind of man would subject his unsuspecting wife to sexually transmitted diseases by having unprotected sex with other men? How dare I commit suicide and leave my wife and children to forever deal with the shame? Over the next few days, Maureen hammered home on those themes.

After a week of agonizing, my HIV test results had not yet come back from the lab. I feared that I might by HIV positive after the experience in the bathhouse. What then? How would I explain such a result? I longed to go home, but was also fearful of the ultimate return to my wife and family.

We had made arrangements months earlier to go to Toronto for a play on the second Friday of my stay in the hospital. I didn't want to disappoint my wife. I had to get a weekend pass. The psychiatrist was adamant—no HIV results—no pass! How could I explain the psychiatrist's reluctance to release me? I had improved since my admission. When it seemed I would not be released, I wrote a long letter to my wife divulging everything! I showed my nurse, Maureen, who alerted the psychiatrist. Both advised me of the folly of such a letter. Surely it would lead to divorce. Was that what I wanted?

I tore up the letter.

I pleaded with the psychiatrist each day. Finally he relented with the admonition "No sex!" while away from the hospital. I could make that work, feigning the effects of my current medication. My wife would be none the wiser. The weekend came and went. I held true to my promise. The truth was I was way too tired to even contemplate it. I returned to the ward Sunday night, hoping this would be my last night there. I could not have foreseen what lay ahead, and the swiftness of what was to follow in the next few weeks, forever changing the lives of myself, my wife and my children.

Once again in the hospital, I awaited the test results and psychiatrist's discharge. Both came early the next morning. My HIV tests were negative!!!!!!!!! The psychiatrist discharged me with the admonition that a second test be taken three months later. I *called my wife to come and pick me up. After fourteen days in the psych ward I was finally free to go home....*

THE HOMECOMING

I didn't return home feeling much different than I did when I was admitted. I had made a promise to Chris never to commit suicide, but other than that all of my previous demons were still there. I pledged to myself that I would refrain from the chat rooms except for connecting with my best friend, Chris.

As soon as I could I emailed Chris to tell him what had happened. Chris had been very worried about my emotional and mental health. He was reassured to learn that I ruled out suicide as an option thanks to his request. I longed to hear Chris' voice and the next day phoned him in North Carolina. It was as if nothing had changed. We both seemed to feel the same way. As usual, we talked about Chris' college, his Tuesday night dart team, his dog, Max, his parents and our feelings for each other.

There were to be only two or three direct conversations between us. In mid-November we talked about Christmas and March Break. I imagined Chris blushing when I told him I was sending him a silver thong. We both laughed about that. Chris was despairing because he had little money for Christmas presents this year. In reality, the only present I longed for was Chris. I knew that would not be, but was unwilling to rule it out.

Around the seventeenth I emailed Chris. When I had no response over the next forty-eight hours, I became concerned. Several emails implored Chris to respond. My old paranoia took over. What had I done to offend him? Finally, on the third day, I received a response, not from Chris, but from his best friend, Michael. Chris had a relapse of his cancer and was in the hospital.

I was devastated!

Chris would recover and everything would be back to normal? The next day, Michael emailed that Chris was semi-conscious most of the day. I asked Michael to mention my name to Chris and tell him I needed him to get better. We had joked when I was discharged from the hospital about going to Hawaii. Now, I asked Michael to remind Chris of the trip. The next day, Michael called again. Chris was now unconscious. Before he slipped away he had asked Michael to tell me to be strong.

The next afternoon Michael emailed once again. Chris had died at one-thirty am CST.

I raged in grief. This couldn't have happened again. Someone I loved unconditionally was taken from me too soon, as my father had been earlier in my life. The date was November 22, 2003, the fortieth anniversary of JFK's assassination in Dallas. Coincidentally, Chris' favorite television programme was Dallas.

Were my tears for Chris or for myself?

I had told my wife about my friendship with Chris a few days earlier. At the same time I told her about Chris' hospitalization. I should have anticipated her indifference. She had heard all about Internet relationships. The husband three doors down the street had left his wife for a woman he had met in North Carolina. Such a fool! Now her own husband was the fool. She suggested I 'get over it'. To me there was no 'getting over it'. This was my beloved Chris. Here I was totally naked emotionally, tears flowing uncontrollably and all she could do was to hug me briefly and tell me to get over it. My hurt was compounded.

I made the decision then to finally tell the truth about my behaviour and attitude of the last few months, but to whom I wasn't sure. Driving down the expressway, I tried calling my ex brother-in-law—the only man with whom I'd ever had a friendship. I nervously dialed his cell, prepared once and for all to share my inner thoughts with this thrice-married man. The phone rang. My nephew answered. My brother-in-law was out of town. Now what? The only other person I could call was the counselor I had visited just once since leaving the hospital. She too was busy and directed me to go home and talk to my wife.

I nervously entered our home and dissolved into tears. She showed no real signs of understanding my devastation. This was a stranger I was grieving after all…someone I'd never actually met.

That evening I was back on the chat lines. I had to connect with someone who could understand my loss. When I did connect, it was with the teacher with whom my wife would discover me in bed the next afternoon.

The masquerade was over, as my emotions erupted at her discovery. She quickly left our home and went back to work. My companion left shortly thereafter expressing his concerns about what had occurred. I wrote her a long letter, packed my clothes and called for a taxi. The moment of reckoning had come!

I wasn't sure what would occur next. In the taxi my head spun with emotions. My secret was out. Surely my actions would result in divorce. I had always felt I would commit suicide if my wife ever found out. That had been the reason for my hospitalization. She'd found out now, but suicide was still not an option, even though it meant I could be with Chris. I would stay at the motel for a few days and try to decide what to do next. Was this to be "the first day of the rest of my life"?

I had purposely selected a motel near my work so as to at least act like things were normal. I packed work boots, jeans and shirts for three days. Beyond that I was uncertain what would occur.

I stopped at the motel office and paid the taxi driver. Using my credit card I booked a room for the week just in case. It wasn't all that bad. It was clean, if dated by the furnishings, but it had a TV and a proper bathroom. I had brought along a few CDs. My clothes were unpacked; my toiletries were placed in the bathroom. At first, I didn't turn on the TV but lay there on the bed listening to Marc Anthony—the songs 'belonging' to Chris and me. Tears flowed unrelentlessly—for Chris and me. What had I done? What would the future hold? How would my daughters accept this? Would they ever allow me to see my three granddaughters and soon to be grandson?

COMING OUT

When I had settled emotionally I took out the small piece of paper in my pocket. On it was written the cell phone number of a new friend; carefully I dialed the number. He answered. After telling him where I was, and why, my friend agreed to come to the motel. I desperately needed companionship at this moment. Maybe it would help me shut out the current realities.

When Mark arrived, I let him in the door. Without hesitation we went straight for the bed and got undressed, beginning to explore each other's bodies. I became lost in the moment. The time went so quickly. We both dressed and faced each other, as my friend offered some advice. He had once been married and had a son. When he came out to his wife she initially accepted her dilemma and allowed him to stay for the sake of the family. Ultimately she asked him to leave after three months. My friend advised me to go home and work things out. After all, we had been married thirty-seven years. A lot of history was evident. At that Mark left and I was left alone to contemplate my future once again.

I lay on the bed for what seemed like hours, Marc Anthony repeating the same song over and over. When it turned dark I decided to get something to eat at the fast food place across the street. Knowing that my wife was home now, I stopped at the phone booth. No answer. I left a message assuring her of my safety. I thought, more than likely, she didn't much care right now. I ordered a burger and sat alone, quietly eating, watching the traffic pass by. I finished, disposed of my garbage and headed back to the motel. Once more I was drawn to the phone booth. I carefully dialed. She answered. What did I want? Did I want to come home? Did I want to see her and talk? I hesitated, but hearing Mark's words, conceded to meeting her at the motel. And then again I waited…She arrived about one half hour later…

My mind had raced. How would she be? I hadn't sensed any anger in her voice, only cold emotion. I opened the door for her to enter and went back to sitting on the chair by the window. She sat on the edge of the bed. Obviously she had read my letter finally divulging the truth about my sexuality, but what more could I say? She was *prepared to work through this; the Christmas holiday season was fast approaching. She had not given the second letter to the two daughters. At this point they had no reason to know. She was prepared to take me home if I wanted to go. I was, but I needed to make it quite clear to her that I had an emotional and physical need for men, as well as women. Could she accept that? She could as long as I was discreet (no more at home hookups) and I had to stay and play safe. She never asked about the type of connections I made, but I figured she presumed at least oral sex. We agreed that marriage counseling was a given. There were too many other issues aside from the sexual ones.*

Shortly after, I packed my clothes and checked out of the motel. I knew full well that she was in the 'power position'. It was evident by her driving me home. For the time being, at least until the New Year, I would be a passenger in her life. She was in the driver's seat, for the rest of our married lives, however long that would be. If she decided that the marriage should be dissolved, I would be the one to, obviously, accept responsibility in telling my daughters and their families.

In one brief month, I had experienced two traumatic experiences—the death of Chris and now this situation. I arrived home to the house we had shared for twenty-five years. When I had left eight hours earlier, I never expected to return except to collect my personal belongings; now here I was. I knew it would never be the same. Later in the evening I emailed my male 'partners' telling them what had occurred...I wasn't sure why.

The situation was tense the first few days. My wife had gone ahead and taken a hard look at our finances in an attempt to see whether or not it would ever be feasible to divorce, or at least, legally separate. Her initial realization was negative. Like most double income couples, our financial resources didn't offer much flexibility. Two cars and two houses were not an option. My wife would normally decline alimony, but under the circumstances I couldn't expect her to reject it. I owed her something. If I had been in her position I would have wanted everything I had, but definitely not me!

We had brief discussions about gay men—nothing of any depth. She did acknowledge that since my coming out she noticed more gays on TV. In Canada, same sex marriage had just become legal in Ontario, so there was a fair amount of public sentiment on both sides of the issue. Then again I had no intention of 'hooking up' in an LTR—long term relationship. All I desired was the occasional physical and emotional bonding.

In this regard I thought myself more bisexual than gay. I enjoyed sex with my wife and was attracted to good looking women, but of the latter, not as much as good looking men. I had been cruising emotionally since my teenage years. That would never change.

I knew I needed help in resolving my sexual doubt and balancing my sexual desires. The counselor I had been seeing since leaving the hospital had not really connected with me. Online I found out about another counselor, private, who dealt with sexual identity issues. At first, I didn't pursue it. One afternoon, while sitting in another coffee shop, I came across an advertisement in the newspaper for the very counselor. I knew I had to try again. Returning to my car, I called the number and made an appointment for the same evening.

This time the counselor did not just sit back and listen to my story. He was a true counselor, even if he had been an ordained Catholic priest at one time. After briefly describing my life prior to that fateful Sunday in November, the counselor questioned, prodded and probed my emotional being.

Mainly we discussed Chris and my prolonged depression surrounding Chris' untimely death. Chris had not caused me to be gay. I already was. What Chris had done was given me the desire and strength to be outted, at least to someone who would not be judgmental. Before Chris' death I never really expected I would come out to my wife. Now I knew I had to; she deserved to know the real reason for my depression, and that she was not at fault in any way. Tears flowed when discussing Chris. I could not hold back. I told the counselor about creating an email address for Chris so I could write him letters after he died. I told him about 'our' music, our phone conversations, etc. In fact, most of the session dealt with my loss of Chris. Chris had been my one and only true friend in my entire lifetime with whom I could share every detail of my life. The counselor suggested that maybe Chris' death had rekindled my emotional void created when my father had died forty years earlier. I had to admit there was probably some truth to that. When my father died, I had locked the emotional door to my heart. Chris reawakened it and then he too was gone.

That evening my wife and I went to a favourite burger joint. Over drinks and burgers I slowly began to unmask myself. I made her realize the impact of Chris' death which she had seriously underestimated. I was able to tell her why we hadn't had sex since my discharge from the hospital. I explained to her why I had previously spent so much time at the computer.

Upon returning home, we went to bed as usual—the same bed. It was too soon to presume we could have any sexual contact, but we did hold each other tenderly until we were ready to fall asleep.

As usual my wife arose early the next day while I languished in bed. While I slept she took the opportunity to watch a video about husbands coming out and to read a book about women in similar situations as hers. When the counselor had given me the book and video I was unsure if she was ready to handle it. I was surprised upon waking that she had actually done it. While enlightening, the video did nothing to allay my fears that I was indeed gay and not bisexual. The doubts persisted.

That evening we discussed what we had seen and read. My wife's bottom line was that I be safe in my dealings with strange men. She wouldn't condone my actions, but, for now, she tried to understand that indeed, her husband was wired for such activities emotionally and that no amount of counseling could change that reality. My hopes were that counseling would allow me to accept those realities of where in my life I currently was. From my readings, I gleaned two very enlightening quotes—

"Now I am lonely for other men and don't know how to find what I want with them"

And

"What I now can confirm is that emotionally and physically I want and need closeness with men and women"

PUTTING THE CHRIS IN CHRISTMAS

Christmas finally arrived—my most dreaded holiday because of my earlier disillusionment when my father had gone off and left us at home. Christmas Eve saw my wife and I gathered at our oldest daughter's home along with the rest of my family, my aging mother and my son-in-law's parents and grandmother.

I felt tense for the whole evening. Strangely, this should have been everything I had ever wanted Christmas to be. It was not to be. We ate dinner and gathered for the traditional gift exchange. Men bought for other men; women bought for women. No names were assigned. Gifts were 'selected' by the participants according to their ages—oldest to youngest.

As I sat in a chair taking all of this in my thoughts turned once again to Chris. I managed to hold back tears as I thought about his tragic loss and for the first time, what Chris' parents and sister must be experiencing in North Carolina that evening—their first Christmas without their beloved son and brother. They no doubt reflected on his recent funeral. According to Chris' friend, Michael, Chris had planned the whole ceremony, including his favourite song, The Magic of Christmas" by Celine Dion. In death Chris had tried to prepare his family and friends for this time. It was so like Chris to leave nothing undone. When he died, his friends found in his backpack the complete arrangements for his own funeral. He must have known it was imminent in his mind, but could he ever have guessed he would be taken so quickly? (Chris' actions prompted me to prepare my funeral arrangements soon after his passing).

As I thought again of Chris' parents and sister I felt a warmth inside. Just prior to Christmas I had contacted Chris' friend, Michael in North Carolina and arranged to have flowers placed on Chris' gravesite. In some small way I deeply wanted Chris to know that our relationship was real. He was loved as he had loved. For weeks prior to sending the money, I had squirreled money away for the money order I sent to Michael in the U.S. I didn't want my wife to know about this. She would just chalk it up to my irrational attachment to the 'stranger' on the Internet. I had been overjoyed when Michael had emailed me "Mission Accomplished". In fact, Michael and the other members of Chris' darts team had gone to the cemetery to place the flowers with my personal note to Chris attached—

> **"If you love someone, set them free. If it's meant to be they will come back to you"**
> **Love always**
> **Bryan**

[Bryan was the name I always used with Chris]

This was a saying my sister-in-law used to display on her living room wall. I had never anticipated it would have personal meaning for me. But, now, here I was saying it to Chris. This wasn't goodbye. There would never be a goodbye. When Chris died I had told Michael that I hoped we would be together someday, and that when I got to Heaven, Chris sure as hell better be waiting for me!

I received my gift, opened it and said the expected "Thanks. Just what I needed—a tool box". Shortly thereafter my wife and I would say our goodbyes and drive home. We unpacked the car. She prepared for bed as usual. I kept my coat on and stepped outside, looking up at the stars—searching for Chris. I knew Chris was up there looking down on all of those who loved him. The tears flowed again. Why? Why did Chris have to go? Did Chris have to go so that I would be forced to live—to live FOR Chris?

The next morning we awoke early, packed the car again and headed for the older daughter's home again—this time to see our granddaughters open Santa's presents. Normally at Christmas my wife and I would pledge not to buy each other gifts. We bought what we wanted all year long. Every year I bought her something special and she would be frustrated because she hadn't gone to any unusual lengths to buy me things other than what I had specifically asked for. I had thought this could be our last Christmas together in light of the recent events. I wanted to give her something significant. She deserved it for what I was putting her through and would continue to put her through. I had purchased a diamond tennis bracelet—well over our personal gift limit. Normally she would open her present, be thrilled, run over and kiss and hug me and rave over the gift. This year she opened it, said an across the room "Thank you" and closed the box without even trying it on. She wanted me to know that this gift was not going to change anything! Gifts exchanged, breakfast over, we gathered up the gifts, packed the car and went home to spend Christmas Day…alone. Both of the girls were spending Christmas at their respective spouse's parents' homes. Things were different this Christmas! Next up would be New Year's Eve. Neither of us worked at our part-time jobs on Boxing Day. We got up, got dressed and went out for breakfast together. On the weekend we were both back at work and life continued on. Although our relationship was amicable, at least to the world, we were both tense beneath the surface.

Just a few days after Christmas I was back on the chat lines—my quest continuing. On the day I was to have my second counseling session, I hooked up with a thirtyish married teacher from a nearby town. We had talked quite a lot on line and he seemed nice enough. As was my now usual practice, we met at a nearby coffee shop and made our initial assessments, before committing to further activity. As it turned out he appeared to have a lot of Chris' qualities; he was good looking with a nice personality and was talkative. He followed me in his car to the nearby short-stay motel which I had earlier booked. After the brief, awkward period, we began to explore each other physically. This time I felt different. This man was so sincere. After our intimate liaison we talked, exchanged email addresses and agreed to meet again. Although he was married, and had children, I wondered if this could be the regular one.

My counseling session focused on the relationship within my own family—parents (mine), my sister and sons-in-law. The counselor was well aware after my first visit of my animosity towards my father. What he explored was my relationship with my mother. There were no tears here. I had come to appreciate my mother's sacrifices on my behalf during my early years without a father. My current relationship was distant. Although she was financially self-sufficient, she lived a modest life in a senior citizens' complex. Because she was legally blind with macular degeneration, she depended on others. She couldn't cook much, so we had arranged at her expense for Meals on Wheels, so that at least five days a week she would have a decent hot meal. My wife did her banking and paid her bills. I was the Power of Attorney on all of her accounts. When I had to, I bought her groceries and took her to her doctor's appointments. She never ventured out alone, content to sit alone in her apartment and watch TV as best she could. Occasionally she would get a whim and actually call me—"I need..." and until I acquiesced, she would persist. I had a hard time hiding my disdain for her. It was, after all, her fault that my father had left the marriage, leaving me fatherless.

Of my older sister, I had to admit being ambivalent. She had never been a presence in my life. She infrequently visited our mother, leaving us to meet mother's needs. Yet, she only lived one hour away! Every three to four months she would come for a few hours, have dinner and leave. She rarely called our mother. For that matter, I didn't either unless I couldn't avoid it. Usually, I conceded to my wife's quiet encouragement *and phoned. In fact, my wife talked with my mother more than I did. After spending a few hours with my mother I would race away—my duty done for a few more weeks.*

My counselor turned his attentions to my relationship with my own daughters and their spouses.

My first child and I had a respectful relationship. She was a strong-willed, capable young woman. Since her marriage I had felt that she had taken on some of her husband's idiosyncrasies. Her opinions reflected his. I knew that each of my daughters loved me as a parent and I loved them as my daughters. Sometimes I had troubles with my oldest daughter. What probably bothered my most was that whenever I offered an opinion and advice, it would be cast aside. It was not unexpected that she would choose her husband's opinions most often. What did I expect her to do? It hurt me to be dismissed in this way. Daughters are supposed to revere their fathers, aren't they? I knew she tried hard to please me in other ways. She always appreciated what I did for her and her family. She was the only daughter to send little 'Thank You' cards for whatever. She truly was like her mother in this regard. She expressed to her mother her concerns about the relationship between her father and her husband. We would never be bosom buddies. Bottom line—we had very little in common. My relationship with him required extra effort and I was working on it. By the end of this counseling session I was able to discern part of my problem—my son-in-law threatened my own sense of masculinity. He was tall and good looking. He was extremely confident in and of himself. He had close male friends which he had had since childhood. Although he currently was unemployed, due to downsizing of his employer, the Canadian government, he would be ultimately successful and very capable whatever he did. Although not a jock he presented himself as one who could be. It just wasn't something he enjoyed. In that way we were alike. I wondered if my son-in-law reminded me too much of my absentee father? Of my other son-in-law I had different feelings.

My younger son-in-law was fairly well grounded. In many ways we were alike. We had simple needs—food, shelter and clothing. There were no pretensions. He was easy going—but certainly not a pushover as a parent to his two young daughters. He accepted responsibility for both girls, even though the oldest child was not his biologically. He had been her 'Dad' since age two. She knew when he spoke she'd better listen. He didn't tolerate insolence or defiance, but held his ground, usually calmly, but firmly.

He was the son of an auto worker and a working mother, with an older sister. He enjoyed his high school years, found a good paying job as a machinist, and settled into living with my youngest daughter and her child. His consistent pleadings to get mar-

ried and adopt her child were rebuffed until well after the birth of their daughter. She reluctantly gave in and allowed for a simple wedding in his family church with a modest reception. At the ceremony each of their daughters was given a 'wedding ring' to symbolize the marriage of all four of them. At the wedding reception, my oldest granddaughter reduced us to tears explaining why she was so happy to have her new Dad 'for real'.

From the beginning we hit it off. Quite often we'd go out for breakfast. We both liked to cook. Whenever my son-in-law needed an extra pair of hands doing something around the house I was there. When my wife wanted something done around our house, she relied on her new son-in-law. He had a talent for those types of things (later on I would be amazed when my older son-in-law also started to develop skills in home repairs). Both sons-in-law were very capable in dealing with computers. My younger son-in-law and I enjoyed golf and took advantage of any opportunity to play. On that fateful weekend in October, prior to my admittance to hospital, we spent the whole day golfing in Michigan, drinking beer and smoking cigars. It was a memory I would always cherish. We made plans then to do this on a regular basis every year.

I anticipated, that although shocked at first, my daughters would accept my coming out. I agonized at how either son-in-law would accept this information. I knew full well that they would all have to be told. The questioned remained—when...and at what cost?

My counselor bluntly told me that I would not be able to hide behind the straight mask forever. My family needed and deserved to be told the truth by their father. At home, my wife and I resolved to tell them after the annual trip to Florida. My oldest daughter was due to give birth to my first and only grandson in mid-January. Now was not the time to share such startling information. I was certainly not a pedophile! My interests were in adult men, not children. I was unsure how my daughters and their spouses would feel about my being with my grandchildren. I wasn't ready for that step yet. Ultimately I decided they would all be told before the trip and not after. I couldn't keep this bottled up inside me for another seven weeks…

The counselor turned his focus to my father and Chris. He concluded that Chris' death had triggered a return to my adolescence—my somewhat distant father, an overbearing and unemotional mother, my longing for male companionship even then. As the waves washed over my psyche I once again unleashed the tears. Why were the only two men I had ever cared about, in my life such a short time? Why did they have to die so young? What would have happened had my father lived?

I had acknowledged writing to Chris even in death. The counselor suggested I continue, but to also attempt to answer my questions to Chris with a written answer that

I might expect of Chris. I had to admit this seemed somewhat strange. Wouldn't Chris' answers be only what I wanted to hear? How could they be objective? I agreed to give it a try.

After the session I returned to the motel, hoping my friend might still be there. He wasn't, so it was time to head home again to my lonely house and once again, my computer and the chat lines.

A NEW YEAR

Between Christmas and New Year's I made no real time connections, although it wasn't for lack of trying. I had sent a note to the teacher, but with his own family and the holidays, there just wasn't time to re-connect.

New Year's Eve, as usual was spent with my wife's closest girlfriend. Whereas I usually barbecued steaks, this year I wasn't in the mood to stay home. We made plans for an early dinner at a nearby restaurant, followed by drinks at home waiting for the ball to drop in Times Square. As the year ended, my wife leaned over with a light kiss. My year from Hell was over, I thought. I had to admit I'd been through a lot. There was still a lot more to come. I quietly went outside and looked up at the stars.

Why Chris? And then the tears...the first of the New Year.
I fell asleep with my CD player and the familiar songs of Marc Anthony...

> **Baby love**
> **Sometimes it's hard for me to tell what I am thinking of**
> **So I try to find a way that I can show you love**
> **What you mean to me**
>
> **It's not enough to give you everything that you were ever dreaming of**
> **I could never find a way that I could pay you love**
> **For all the things you do**
> **'Cause when my life gets crazy**
> **The only one who comforts me is you.**
>
> **When I'm feeling all alone**
> **When I'm searching for someone I can run to**
> **I reach for you**
> **When I need a hand to hold**

Or a place where I can feel what love can do
I reach for you
Needing you
Is something that I've really gotten used to
I can't imagine being here with no one else
No one but you.

What I found
Is it doesn't get much better than when you're around
Having you is all I need when I get down
You pull me through

'Cause when my life
Gets crazy
The only one who comforts me is you.

And...

I used to try
To set aside
Some time for being lonely

So many times
I prayed to find
Someone like you to hold me

I'm not alone
I just simply close my eyes
And sing my song
And I am home
Loving where I belong

Do you believe in loneliness?
I do now that's where I found you and I'll never let you go

When all I knew was onlyness
There you were
With you around
Who's lonely now?

I feared the night
But now it's mine
'Cause something's out there for me

Let's take our time
I'm satisfied
With having you to own me

All I know is that when I think of you
I'm not alone
I just simply close my eyes
And sing my song
And I am home
Loving where I belong.

Before the New Year was even a week old I met another friend. This one was also married, but somewhere in his mid-thirties. I had come to realize that married men had to be much more discreet. After arguing as to who would pay for the motel, I reluctantly caved in. We met in the same motel as I had been to previously. There was something about the mirrors on the walls and ceiling that added to the pleasure of the moment.

This particular guy was an engineer by profession—tall and fairly good looking. He was what seemed like a really nice guy, although not too talkative. After he was 'released' he was satisfied to leave. Even still he was appealing as a potential regular player. No commitments…just a fun time for both of us.

After my next scheduled counseling session I started to attend a once a week group session. I had high expectations of meeting some men, like myself, who were juggling marriage and their desires to be with other men. Such was not to be the case.

Arriving at the meeting I noticed a twenty something standing on the steps in a long, cloth coat. Must be one of the group. When the time came I entered the building with the other man and headed to the meeting room. Only two other men showed for the session. Each person introduced themselves and explained briefly why they were there and where they were at in their lives. Each of us had come out to various persons. The young man was unattached at the moment, I assumed because he was essentially a 'flamer', who disliked 'breeders'...those normal people who so desperately wanted to reproduce to extend their lineage. He ranted on about his relationship with his parents and a sister. If only he would shut up...

The next oldest guy, an architect in his early thirties was at first very quiet. His eastern European background made coming out especially difficult. Most of his friends knew he was gay; his parents were the exception. His mother was content to believe he was busy building his career and had no time for a wife and children. He had dated earlier and become engaged. After six years, his girlfriend had realized marriage was not to be. He looked way too conservative compared to the 'flamer'. He was also fairly shy about himself, almost painfully.

The third guy, in his early forties I presumed was kind of in the middle of the first two. Slim looking, pleasant appearance, he had been married but was now divorced and living with his partner.

The four of us slowly started to open up in this uneasy setting. Before we knew it, an hour and a half had passed. The counselor went around the room asking each man to commit to some further action during the week.

The 'flamer' said he would quit smoking and ease up on his drinking. [Fat chance, I thought.] The architect pledged to deal with his own work load. I forgot what the third man said.

I agreed to finally try dealing with my grief over Chris by attempting the question and answer strategy the counselor had suggested. Of the entire group I was the only one who made a decision relating to my present status. Maybe at this stage in life I was growing more desperate. The other guys had lots of life ahead of them.

I was glad the session had ended; after all, none of these men would ever appreciate my situation. At fifty-eight years of age I was trying desperately to be true to myself. No younger, single man would understand the sacrifices I was making in order to remove my lifelong mask. I had stated during the session that I was coming out, but I wondered—at what cost? I couldn't imagine. Would the cost be worth it?

The following day I was feeling particularly lonesome again. I was scheduled for a meeting with my former brother-in-law to discuss a pending business matter. I trolled the chat lines until I once again found the engineer. Sure he'd like to hook up again.

Today? Sure. Before we broke off the conversation, a third guy chimed in. How about a threesome? I pondered the experience. I asked the engineer if he knew how old the third guy was. Twenty-seven. The meet was arranged at the usual motel. Off I set, ignoring my previous engagement. This was more important right now.

When I arrived at the motel, the twenty-seven year old was there…waiting with…his bicycle. Rather odd I thought for a twenty-seven year old. I entered the room and shortly thereafter the young man chained his bicycle, knocked on the door and entered somewhat apprehensively. After all, I was old enough to be his father. I sensed the young man was anxious as we waited for the engineer. I was shirtless. The young man remained clothed. We watched some mindless TV, commenting occasionally. When the engineer had not arrived yet, I stroked the young man's leg. Didn't he want to get more comfortable? A timid "Sure", followed by inaction. At this moment the engineer arrived, said his hellos and proceeded to answer his beeping pager. He could not stay. Business called. "Have fun", he said as he quickly departed. Now it was just the two of us. There was no turning back. The young man took off his shirt and lay on the bed. Very shortly we were engaged in the regular routine. The young man appeared to finally relax and enjoy the encounter.

One and a half hours later we got dressed and sat and talked. This was different. Would he like a coffee? "Sure", replied the young man, who I know knew as Dan. For the next hour we sat and talked. Dan had been married, but separated. He had two small children. He lived with two straight guys (so he told me). He only saw his kids on weekends. He had worked in heating and cooling but was laid off—looking for work. Not this kind! We talked like two good buddies. Could this be the regular guy? I was starting to sound like the baby chick in the children's story book who thinks every animal could be his mother. I found myself thoroughly enjoying our time, regretting I had to leave to pick up my wife at work. And then I remembered my brother-in-law. Oh well, too late now!

My wife inquired as to how my meeting had gone. "I didn't make it", I said. My brother-in-law had a dentist appointment that ran late. When we got home there was a phone message. "Sorry I missed you. Call me ASAP". This boat didn't float. I was caught in another lie. For the rest of the evening there was an icy silence between us which continued in our bedroom. Even though my wife knew about my sexual preferences we continued to sleep together and have occasional sex. Not this night!

I put on my headset, listening to the songs of Josh Groban, which by this time I had memorized. Then I listened to Marc Anthony again. I hoped my wife didn't hear me crying when I played the songs reminding me of Chris.

All my life
I've followed signs
On many a road

Tried to find
What was right?
And do what I'm told

But sometimes
You cross the line
And never can go back home

I've been here
And I've been there
Always on the go

Looking for
Something more
To call my own

Up to now
I have found
That life as a whole was cold

'Cause I've never belonged

I wanna be free
And live my life without warning
I wanna finally see
What it's like on the other side
I wanna be free
"Cause a new day is dawning

I wanna be me
I wanna show the world I'm alive

Who's to say
I need change
And I am not what I'm not

Look at me
And what you see
Has been through a lot

Now it's time
For me to find
What love's all about
And all that I've lived without.

I lay awake most of the night pondering my next move. When morning finally came, I awoke, told my wife the truth of my whereabouts the previous afternoon and proceeded to tell her I was going to my brother-in-law's. I would tell him the truth about where I had been, no matter the cost. My proclivity for relationships with men was making me dysfunctional. I wasn't handling the situation well. I needed to remove more of my mask or risk becoming a sexual addict.

Before I left, I showed my wife the picture of Chris. He was real after all. He had lived and died, but somewhere in between he had made a huge impact on my life. I drove to my brother-in-law's plant. He was not there, nor was he at home. With my emotions peaking, I couldn't go home until I found him. Calls went unanswered where I thought he might be. I started to drive around, hoping that he would eventually show up somewhere. As I was driving I had a sudden urge to visit my father's gravesite in the nearby town. I had been wearing my father's signet ring since Chris' death. The insignia "C" could represent either Chris, or my father, whose name also began with a "C". In this way I was honouring both men who had played significant though varied roles in my life.

While driving my mind went back to the funeral arrangements I had written and placed in my wallet. Ever since a trip to Phoenix when the girls were young, I had made it known that I wanted to have my ashes dispersed there in the mountains when

I died. Now I realized what really was needed were for my ashes to be interred in my father's grave. Perhaps in death we would achieve some closure.

Something made me turn around. I HAD to find my brother-in-law. Heading back into the city I received a call from my nephew's cell phone. He was right behind me in his truck. Where was I going? He gave me his father's cell phone number and I dialed. Please answer. I need to see you NOW! It's very important.

Upon arrival at his plant I entered to find my brother-in-law engaged in conversation with the production manager. After exchanging pleasantries I told my brother-in-law we needed to talk in private. The walk back to his office felt like I was heading to the gallows. I was about to share my sordid story with the only other person I considered a friend. This wasn't going to be easy...

As we sat down I blurted out "I'm having an affair". When my brother-in-law started to smile I said, "It's not what you think. This is who I am having an affair with". I showed him the picture of Chris and stammered "I am gay".

Shocked disbelief showed on my brother-in-law's face as I shared the entire story—the adolescent sexual activity, the norms of marriage and kids, career and finally the long time loneliness and subsequent hospitalization for the so-called depression or chemical imbalance depending on whose story you heard. I told him of my love for Chris and Chris' untimely death; I told him about the motel connection the previous day. I broke down as my brother-in-law calmly stated "You're still you. That hasn't changed". My brother-in-law felt my pain at that moment and came to place his hand on my shoulder—his gay brother-in-law's shoulder. Was I playing safe? Was I being careful? He knew I was not exactly street smart as was he. The conversation concluded and I got up to leave having now acknowledged to two people my gayness. I was relieved at this disclosure but knew my biggest challenge was still my two daughters and their families. Upon returning home, my brother-in-law was once again on the answering machine. "How about dinner, Sunday?" I guess he was trying to make things seem normal...

Over the next few days I regained some degree of functionality. The Christmas decorations were finally put away in the attic. I tidied up the house and made dinner, something I hadn't much felt like doing of late. Just maybe I was making progress? I still went to work regularly, did a good job and acted as though nothing had changed. I couldn't, however, get past the idea that my one closest friend at work was still in the dark about me. I wasn't sure if or when I could tell him the truth. My friend knew I was distressed; my marriage was suffering, but he never once suspected the real cause was my sexual identity crises...or so I thought at this time.

I explained to my counselor about my brother-in-law's reaction to my disclosure. I reiterated my conflict—doubts about my sexuality versus desires for male companionship—physical and emotional. The counselor applauded my disclosure. I shared the photograph of Chris and of my own father. I had them both laminated just that morning. They were both handsome men. Both had died too soon. They had both left me just when I needed them most. Was Chris the cause of the reawakening of my adolescence? Was I looking for Chris to take my father's place in some strange twist of fate? Chris, after all, provided the paternal wisdom of which I had always been deprived.

The counselor asked me to keep a dream diary—a standard counseling practice. I was amazed at the images I recorded—reconstructing buildings, reaching the end of a bridge with no land in sight, retreating to a safer road. I wasn't sure I was interpreting my dreams objectively. All signs pointed to my dreams being subjective. What I read into them was what I was experiencing. The dreams seemed all so prophetic.

On my way home that evening I made the decision. I would not tell my children until we returned from Florida. At nine months pregnant my oldest daughter wouldn't be prepared for the revelation. If I couldn't tell one, I couldn't tell either. That evening I sat at the island in the kitchen finally doing the question and answer technique with Chris as instructed by the counselor. I wasn't sure that Chris' answers were what I really thought Chris would say or what I wanted to hear.

I continued to talk with other men in the local chat room. Each time I logged on I hoped either the teacher or the engineer would be there. If not them then perhaps Dan. Any of the three made me feel comfortable—Dan because he was closer to Chris' age and seemed interested in more than sex. This one could be a real friend. My hopes were quickly diminished when none of the three were ever in the room when I was surfing.

The following week I had a scheduled doctor's appointment. When I last visited the doctor, who I'd known for over ten years, I had dropped the bombshell about needing a second HIV test to verify the first negative result from the hospital. This time I hoped the results would be the same. If the test came back positive my world would totally collapse, of this I was absolutely sure. All of the masks would be dropped. My life would literally explode.

Entering the office I explained to the nurse what I was there for—test results and prescription renewals and a possible hepatitis vaccination. I had read that gay men were potential hepatitis cases and was very determined to do all I could to prevent this happening to me. The doctor entered. I immediately related the truth to him. The disbelieving doctor confirmed I was still HIV-, and yes, I should have the hepatitis shots.

After renewing my prescriptions, the doctor took the opportunity to chastise me. How could I do this after thirty-seven years of marriage? I had a good wife and family. Was I ready to throw that away? I knew then that this doctor might never understand my situation.

At the counselor's that afternoon I related my experience with the doctor. He wasn't surprised by my doctor's reaction. This was not a curable disease, but a predetermined lifestyle which I had tried to push away all these years. Was the sex with men an attempt to get the emotional connection or was there something more? Did I have to be either straight or gay? Was there no middle road—bisexuality? The counselor encouraged me to answer my own questions. The tears lessened this time, as I related how I had changed my funeral plans to include burial with my father.

The next day was the scheduled group session but it was postponed by the first heavy snowstorm of the winter. I had looked forward to it, although I didn't particularly feel comfortable with the 'flamer'. When it was cancelled I was truly disappointed. The next day as I prepared for work, I was stopped by my wife at the front door. She needed me to tell her girlfriend. She wanted to be able to talk to someone about this. After two months she was finally ready to remove her mask. She had nothing to be ashamed of. She had always been a loving and supportive wife and a devoted mother. She hadn't created a gay husband. I could and would not refuse her request. We scheduled a dinner for the next evening at our home. I was about to come out to yet another person, but still not my daughters.

This was not a casual friend. She was a friend to both of us. We had all been brought together when her husband died the week before my wife's sister in December 1986. I introduced her often as 'my second wife'—a standard joke. We attended shows together, went on vacations and usually ate or had coffee together a couple of times a week. We truly enjoyed each other's company.

As we sat down to a dinner of salad and pasta, my adrenalin was rushing. How would I break the news? When would I tell in the course of the evening? How would she react? After finishing our dinner I knew it was time to tell. I jumped into the conversation with my revelation...

When I had been hospitalized it was not because of a chemical imbalance. I had been suicidal! I was suicidal because I was having a long time online affair with a twenty-three year old man in North Carolina. I had also been seeing other men locally. Shortly after my chat line 'friend' had died, I was caught by my wife in bed with another man.

I looked up to gauge her reaction, and then looked across at my wife. There were no tears. I continued to explain that we were staying in our marriage, at least for the foreseeable future. I was gay. I wasn't going to change. I explained why we had taken so long to tell her the truth—my wife wasn't ready until now. As I got up to leave the house to allow them to talk privately, our friend got up and gave me a big hug, followed by a hug for my wife. I put on my coat and went out for a coffee. I was relieved. It had gone fairly well. Most of all I was glad that my wife now had someone with whom she could share her concerns. I had successfully scaled two mountains…Mount Everest (my daughters) would still have to wait seven weeks.

That evening I went back on the computer hoping one of my three guys would be there. They weren't. Nor was Chris' friend Michael, in person or by email.

I had chatted with Michael for over an hour and a half the previous night. We continued to talk about Chris, but slowly, each of us began to reveal more of himself to the other. I couldn't help but feel like I was talking to Chris. Conversation came easily. Michael sent me a couple of humorous pictures of himself. We talked about Michael's girlfriend, the Tuesday Night Darts League, college, the American draft system and Canadian beer. I tried very hard not to dwell on Chris. I knew Michael was still grieving the loss as was I. (This was not the appropriate time to tell Michael about the sexual nature of Chris and my conversations. As far as I knew, Michael was straight. I didn't want to 'out' Chris at this point). Twice I said goodbye, but Michael wouldn't stop chatting. Finally the chat came to an end. Before saying goodbye I told Michael about the 'gift' Chris had given me when he died—his best friend, Michael. The latter was at a temporary loss for words. I logged off after saying that Michael was 'my new best guy'. Almost instantly I wanted to retract those words. How would Michael feel about the reference? After all, Chris was Michael's 'boy'. Would Michael see this as a rebounding situation? Chris was gone. Was I moving on to Michael? What would Michael think? I had no desire to replace Chris; all I wanted was to have Michael as a close friend. Beyond that I had no physical interest in him whatsoever.

I quickly logged back on explaining my paranoia over the remark I had made. "Don't be offended Michael! Please don't misinterpret my remarks. Email me back and tell me you understand."

I wanted and needed Michael's reply, but it was not forthcoming. I agonized over the faux pas. The next night I still had not heard back. Had I blown it with Michael? Please no! I couldn't lose my only direct link with Chris now. Please God!

Early the next morning I was awakened by a phone call from my oldest daughter. Her water had broken and she was headed to the hospital to deliver our grandson. I thought back to the birth of my second grandchild three years previous. How far I had come, yet I had still not found joy except for my too brief relationship with Chris. Was there no living person who could help me in my quest? Was I destined to be a Don Quixote? Was my dream impossible? What if there was never to be a someone? My mind reeled. Every day the cost of my coming out was mounting. I felt momentarily overwhelmed and retreated into the now familiar music which Chris and I had shared—

"...when my life gets crazy, the only one who comforts me is you".

I had been too naïve to imagine what would happen in the next twenty-four hours. My daughter delivered a healthy, seven pound, fourteen ounce son, whom they called Jack. I wasn't really exhilarated because it made me think of Chris. My friend would never experience fatherhood. Chris and I had jokingly discussed the fact that if the two of us would ever get together, Chris would be a grandfather at twenty-three years of age! We had laughed at the image…

The next evening, after visiting my new grandson, we returned home and I again headed for the computer. I had heard someone on the radio talking about the merits of a search engine called 'Google'. I had searched Yahoo.com for Chris' obituary notice to no avail. For some reason I decided to try Google. Within minutes I had found Chris' web page. There was a moment of excitement. My heart raced at the thought that I had found Chris' legacy. But wait a minute! That picture was NOT Chris….

THE REALITY

I scanned through the page. There was information about his birth, his family and his friends. In some of the pictures was the person I thought was Chris. How could that be? There was Chris' friend, Michael. As I moved to the end of the page, I noted the date—12/29/03 this couldn't be. Chris had died on November 22, 2003, didn't he?

Chris' parents were shown on the site. I decided to type in their name to see if I could find anything else. Within seconds I had Chris' home address and phone number. Strangely they were the same as Michael's. What was going on? I quickly emailed Michael and cc'd Chris' hotmail address…

> *You've probably already received my previous message about finding Chris' homepage. I was so excited. At last I knew more about Chris. His death left me more devastated than you can probably know. I truly cared for whoever I was writing to. I searched for weeks to find a death notice and could not understand why I found none. Now that I've found the homepage, I am really confused. Can someone please answer the following questions—*
>
> 1. *Is Chris dead?*
> 2. *If he is dead why does the date on the home page show December 2003?*
> 3. *Who is Michael?*
> 4. *Why are Chris and Michael's addresses the same?*
> 5. *Was this a case of someone getting in too deep and needing to end the relationship?*
>
> *You need to know I still shed tears for the Chris I knew and loved. All I want is the truth at last. I bear no grudge for what has happened. If Chris or ? does not want to hear from me again, please be man enough to tell me directly and I will fade away.*
>
> *I miss the man I knew and loved, but don't leave me out here not knowing the truth. I would rather know that my guy was alive, so I could truly move on.*

I would rather not have to phone his parents, especially if I am off base here. I wouldn't want to hurt them, but I need to know!

That evening my wife and I went to our neighbour's for dinner. I couldn't wait to get home to see who, if anybody would reply. As I clicked on MSN there was a reply from Michael, Chris' friend—

Okay—here we go. First of all, my name is Michael. I am Chris' best friend. No, Chris is not dead yet, but he will be very soon. He is currently in hospital in Minnesota. Although I don't feel right about what's going on here, with Chris dying, I can't very well not do something that he wants me to do. I guess I don't know everything that went on between the two of you, but I kinda got the jist I know Chris lied to you about what he looked like, but then so did I when I sent you the picture—that is actually our friend xxxx and he lives in Chicago. But you know all about lying about what you look like, or so I'm told. When people get into these chat room situations they lie—you did, he did and now I've done it. Chris does care for you and that's why he asked me to do this in the first place. I've actually been working on Chris' website for him since he's in the hospital, so that's why the dates are the way they are. Pretty much everything Chris told you was true; I've done most of the lying here. Chris just wanted you to think that he was dead because he knew he'd never talk to you again and he just wanted you to be able to move on. He didn't stop talking to you because of some dumb reason; he really is dying and he knew that once he left this town, he'd never come back. The address that you sent the money order to is Chris' parents' house. I didn't want you to send it, but I couldn't not let you do it, otherwise you'd figure out what was going on. The money was used for flowers; however, me and the rest of the dart team delivered them to him personally. That was the last time I saw Chris. I intercepted the mail at his house because his parents were in MN with him, so I knew it would be safe for the mail to go there without someone else getting it. Chris' family has no idea about what's going on here or what was going on between you and him. I saw in your email that you were thinking about contacting them DO NOT DO THAT. Hearing something like that would really hurt them—although you probably have lost most of the respect that you had for him; if you have any left you will leave his family out of this. Go through me with whatever information you need to know. I know you can't trust me because of all of the lies I've told you, but I give you my word that I'll tell you the truth about the situation from now on. You obviously didn't trust me anyways, because you've been doing a hell of a lot of digging for information about Chris. Looking up addresses and phone numbers—going into websites—I am truly very very sorry about all this. At the beginning I didn't think it would be a big deal and I figured that once I told you Chris was dead, you'd just go away. After the first time I *talked to you, I knew that you cared for Chris quite a bit and I wanted to end it right there and then. I couldn't because that is what Chris wanted—I am not sure what made him think that this would be the best way, but what's done is done. Like I said, I'm really sorry about all this, but please—if you want more info, go through me with emails and MSN Messenger. Please leave Chris' family out of it. Bryan, you're gonna have to let him go anyway-he's not going to be around much longer—I'm telling you. Just email me back or whatever and hopefully we can tie up the loose ends with whatever else you want to know. I'm sure you're mad and hurt, but don't do anything stupid—try to keep a level head about what you plan on doing. This is just a warning—I know you have the addresses and phone numbers of Chris' family because you've done a lot of digging, but know this—I love Chris like a brother and I love his family—they're going through enough right now, so don't do anything to complicate the situation. If you do, know that I have your information too, and if you choose to do something dumb like trying to contact his family I can certainly reciprocate and I won't hesitate to do so. I know that sounds really mean of me to say, but I don't want this situation to get any worse than it already is. Just email me back and we can talk about it more, okay? Talk to you later…*

Michael

How can one be so happy, sad, angry and humiliated all at the same time? I was blown out of the water by Michael's revelation. I was overjoyed that Chris was indeed alive, yet that meant my grief had been premature after all. I didn't hate Chris for trying to spare me, forcing me to move on sooner. Would I endure a second round of grief when the moment of his death actually came? Was Chris suffering? I hoped not. Everything seemed to collapse around me. Chris was alive, but indeed dying in a hospital in Minnesota.

The Chris whose picture I had in my wallet was not really Chris, not that it really mattered. It was the inner Chris I had been attracted to. I was glad that Chris had seen the flowers in life. As for threatening to contact Chris' family that was an idle threat. I would never divulge my relationship with Chris to his parents. I would never hurt Chris.

As for Michael, I truly felt sorry for him. He was Chris' best friend. He was only doing what Chris had thought right. He got caught up in the moment—Chris' unconsciousness, his funeral service written on a piece of paper in his backpack, right down to the music played. How many times had I listened to Celine Dion's **Magic of**

Christmas *and cried over Chris? Like me, Michael would eventually face the true reality of Chris' passing.*

I printed out Michael's letter, reading it over and over, digesting every detail. At first, I wasn't sure how to reply, but I did so in an unemotional, mature manner. I closed by asking Michael to IM me later that night. When no response was received before I went to bed, I IM'd Michael asking him to be online the next evening between eight and ten o'clock. We had to talk. I still had questions about Chris. I shut down the computer, tore up the pictures of Chris' friend in my desk and in my wallet and went to bed.

In bed, I showed my wife the letter. She read it carefully and asked, "Is this going to set you back again?" I confidently replied in the negative, but knew in my heart that when Chris really died all of the emotions would probably resurface. What I desperately needed now was to talk to my counselor, but that would have to wait forty-eight hours until my next (and last) appointment before heading to Florida the following week. My mind and heart were in limbo. Ironically I needed to talk with Chris now more than ever before. So much had happened since Chris' feigned death in November. If only we could speak? I knew we never would. A part of me died that night. Chris would never have imagined in his wildest dreams how much he had impacted my life. I turned off the lights, put on my headset and tried to sleep, mentally going over Michael's letter. Why? At the same time, I prayed—"Please let Chris live!" I should have felt joy knowing he was not dead. My heart was icing over again on that cold January evening, just as it had forty years ago when my father died.

I managed to get through the next day. I hurried home after work to see if Michael had emailed me. Yes!!!! I quickly opened the letter. Michael was apologetic about his idle threat as well, but he was terrified that I would contact Chris' parents. I would try to IM him later. I guessed we were both breathing more easily now, even though we had huge heartaches over Chris. Michael was in for a very difficult time. Maybe in our chatting he would be better able to prepare himself for Chris' real death.

Michael didn't IM or email me that evening. Sitting at the computer up came a message from the teacher. I was glad for the distraction. The teacher was coming into the city for a meeting the next afternoon. Could we possibly meet? Well, I wasn't working. I would have jumped through the proverbial hoops to hook up again. We agreed to meet. I was pleased we would be able to meet before my wife and I headed to Florida in six more days. I juggled my to-do list and headed for bed.

While waiting to have new tires put on my car, my mind scheduled my day until I met with the teacher. The hours went by slowly. First would come the last meeting with my counselor. The counselor would no doubt be shocked by Michael's revelation. Where would we go from here? For the next seven weeks I would be on my own with my thoughts. I sat in my car outside the counselor's office waiting for my appointed time. I re-read the question and answers I had done, answers that reflected what I knew Chris would say. Knowing Chris was still alive now, it felt strange. Then again, maybe these were the answers Chris was 'communicating' from his hospital bed. It had been an interesting exercise after all. Right now I wasn't feeling teary eyed. I would be sorrowful if and when Michael notified me of Chris' passing, but I knew I had to shed the grief blanket. Spring would be here soon. It was time to wean myself from the security of Chris. Let him go. Be there for Michael when the time came, but I couldn't continue to dwell in this emotional house of sorrow. Chris would always be a positive part of me. But here and now I had to move on…finally, fulfilling Chris' wish for me. "May God bless you Chris as you begin your next journey…umh…?

With that I headed in for my appointment.

This one was different. I felt oddly pumped up. I recalled the week's events as I always did, starting with finally coming out to my wife's friend. And then it was time to share Michael's letter. As the counselor read, he exclaimed, "Oh no!" at the line stating that Chris was alive. He continued to read to the end, stopping at the name, Bryan, the only name my online friends ever knew for me. He read about Michael's idle threats should I ever try to contact Chris' parents.

When he finished he asked the expected question, "How do you feel?" I replied "I'm alright with this. I've already grieved for Chris. It doesn't matter that the picture wasn't him. I loved him for what he was to me."

As for Michael I related my sense of sorrow for him; he had lived out Chris' death online; his reality had yet to come, when Chris finally died.

As for the whole charade, all three of us played a part based on good intentions—Chris, Michael and me. There could be no animosity here.

Generally the counselor was surprised at my cool demeanor. His client had been correct all along. Chris was more than an online friend. He was the vehicle for my facing my own emotional realities. Fate had brought Chris into my life just when I needed him most! About this whole period of time, since meeting Chris, how did I feel? In a single word, I answered, "Taller." I was only five feet, six inches tall. How could I feel taller? After pausing a few minutes I responded that essentially I was emotionally taller than at any time in my entire life. The last six months had taken their toll, but I felt more acceptance of myself; I no longer hid behind all of the masks of normalcy—all the time living with a secret. I had survived the guilt over possibly being HIV infected. I had finally started to come out to friends—all at my own pace.

I still had three important people to tell—my daughters (and their spouses) and my friend at work. I had almost told him the last week, but at the last moment he had brought along a friend. The opportunity was lost for now. The counselor wondered how I'd react when my friend dismissed me for being gay. My answer, "It will be his loss, not mine." I was still myself in every way except my sexual orientation. If my friend couldn't see it that would be his problem…or so I believed at that moment.

I left the counselor's office feeling good. I wasn't yet 'joyous', but there was potential after all these years of searching.

The next hour and a half was spent in the company of the teacher. We had arranged to meet once again at the motel. For my part I had told my wife that I wouldn't be right home after the counseling session. She never asked why. This meeting went better than the first. We slowly undressed each other and began exploring. It was the teacher's idea for the joint shower. Together, soaping each other was so stimulating. I imagined myself at the gym, this time my fantasy was being fulfilled. We dried off and returned to our previous activity on the bed. It ended too soon for me, but my wife expected me home by six o'clock.

On my way home, I concocted the story of visiting my father's grave. She was not amused when I walked in at 6:07 p.m. How come my cell phone was off? Where had I been? I knew she thought I had been with another man. I could sense her anger and resentment. Was this how she was always going to react now? I had made it clear back in November that I would continue seeing men. When did she think I would connect? Had she fooled herself into thinking my counseling would make this go away? Her husband was gay for God's sake! When your husband is gay that means he seeks out the company of other men. I couldn't come right out and tell her about each liaison. I didn't want to shove my gayness in her face. After dinner, I couldn't just say, "Oh, I'm going out for dessert now." LOL (to use Internet terms—Laughing out loud) That would be pretty crass…

After telling her I had visited the grave she started to come around. At least she started to respond with more than a single word.

I checked my email before heading out to see my new grandson. No reply from Michael. Oh well, he'll get in touch when he can. It was darts night in North Carolina. I knew he'd eventually check in.

When my wife was settled into bed, I went back to the computer and the chat lines. As I clicked on I saw the name of a former acquaintance. I sent him an IM alert, to which he responded. Mindless chatting was followed by some serious communication. From my perspective Marco was a potential 'regular'. We seemed to enjoy each other on our previous two encounters. Since the second there had been no common time to re-connect. Both of us were frustrated while trying to search for a time and date for another meet.

It was always later at night when Marco started to chat. I never felt comfortable enough yet to tell my wife I was going out at 10:00 p.m. My friend was frustrated. On several previous occasions I had told him that late nights were not possible. What didn't he understand?

Growing tired of trying to force his hand (no pun intended) I suggested we end the chat. If he really wanted me he need only call. The ball was left in his court. I hoped that he would come around soon. I wanted it to be, in spite of our age difference. This man was wise beyond his years. Ironic, that's what Chris' mother said about him…

I awoke the next morning feeling different—more peaceful. I had a scheduled doctor's appointment, along with my mother. I always dreaded these days with her. On most occasions I barely spoke to her, feigning boredom. This time was different. We actually carried on a conversation all the way there. At the doctor's I joked with the young nurse who was giving me my second hepatitis shot. On the way home our conversation continued. At one point I felt today was the day to tell her that I was gay. I erased the idea. I got as far as explaining I felt better. I pointed out my counselor's office. She remarked that I seemed better today. Did someone flick a switch while I slept? I felt jovial and started singing in the car after I dropped her off at her apartment. Who was this person? What was he doing in my body? I felt taller indeed! A smile came across my face…progress at last. Strains of Josh Groban's "You Raise Me Up" played on the radio—

> *You raise me up*
> *So I can stand on mountains*
> *You raise me up*
> *To cross the stormy seas*
> *I am strong*
> *When I am on your shoulders*
> *You raise me up*
> *To be more than I can be*

Was this Chris' present to me?

Indeed for the next few days I felt better. Maybe the medications were finally kicking in.

Prior to my weekly group session I connected once again with Dan—this time just for a coffee. I felt really good sitting there with him He had just told his father and a brother that he was indeed gay. We talked about how he felt, what his plans were and about his young children. Their mother had custody. She also had their van and any money she could squeeze out of him. When it was time to go we drove to a nearby gas station to fill up my car. I stopped at the ATM machine taking out forty-five dollars—five for the Dan's cigarettes and forty so he could buy some groceries as the kids were coming to see him on the weekend. I was always a sucker for kids, especially my own grandchildren. I dropped my friend off at his home and quickly headed for the counselor's office.

That night, at counseling, I related what had occurred over the last couple of weeks. There were four guys this week, the three from the previous week and a new one. The new one was six feet tall, well-built, but had a slight speech impediment, which I assumed was the result of a broken jaw. Indeed as each of us took a turn at revelations, the newcomer confirmed his condition…injured in a pub brawl…

The 'flamer' was much more subdued tonight. The architect was his usual shy evasive self. The sales rep sat back silently smirking while the new guy related all the sordid details of his fight and subsequent arrest. It was the sales rep who decided to ask questions about Chris' death. I confidently explained the turn of events, concluding I was cool with it and ready to move on. My period of mourning was officially over…or so I thought then…

At the computer that night I looked for a message from either Michael, the teacher or Dan. There were none and I headed off to bed.

I worked all the next day. Just before home time, Dan called me. "Could we meet after 6:30?" "Yeh, sure." "I'll call you." I quickly went home and showered. Six-thirty passed. At six-forty-five I phoned. No answer. I headed for the nearest coffee shop by his house to wait for his call. At seven fifteen I headed slowly home. What a fool I was!

I had only ever dated one girl—my wife. I had never experienced emotional rejection from the opposite sex. Yet, now that I had come out as a gay man, I felt the sting of such rejections. I really liked this guy. I was disappointed at the turn of events. He never called and never emailed. I was learning first hand how rejection felt.

I had a lot of errands the next day—banking, groceries, and drug store. We were getting ready for the Florida trip. This year would be different. We were heading south for seven weeks. With all that happened since last year, I was very apprehensive. I refused to pack until the last moment. The guys at the group wished me well—seven weeks of celibacy, but then again time to reflect. The sales rep gave me a big hug of support. I was surprised—it felt so good. My counselor offered his email address in case I needed to connect while away.

While I was at the grocery store, Dan called. He apologized saying there had been a problem with his ex-wife and the kids. How about this afternoon? I didn't hesitate to say yes, but as the afternoon moved into the evening once again no response. I sent him a terse note "Sorry we couldn't connect. Hope all is well. Keep in touch". With that I signed off the computer until sometime later.

I logged on checking to see if my work friend had sent a reply to my earlier letter. We had met once again for breakfast and once again he had invited another person. Damn. I had spent most of the night previous deliberating over how to tell him that I was gay. When the opportunity didn't arise, I knew I would be forced to tell him in writing. This couldn't wait until I returned from Florida.

COMING OUT AT WORK

In my letter I removed all of the previous masks—truth about my hospitalization, the truth about Chris, truth about being emotionally and physically attracted to men. I hoped my only friend since childhood would understand. I couldn't lose him right now. I had already lost too many men in my life—my father, my great grandfather, my father-in-law, Chris, probably Michael and Dan. I couldn't lose this guy. My counselor had warned me. I was so determined that if he dumped me, it would be his problem and not mine. Realistically I couldn't convince myself that this was the case.

There was no immediate reply. I was saddened but pragmatic…maybe tomorrow. With my wife out for the evening, I continued to work on my 'novel' which I had begun the past summer. I always found this somewhat cathartic. In my present state the ending was still unclear. I knew there were many chapters yet to be written.

My last shift at work was the Saturday. My friend didn't work weekends so I wasn't worried about facing him after the revealing letter. It was a good day. I exceeded my expected sale goals for the day and surpassed my previous week's sales as well (I would later receive two commendations for my work in this department). My youngest daughter's two children were sleeping over for the last time prior to our leaving. Later that night my oldest daughter phoned. She was getting emotional about our leaving so soon after the birth of her son. She knew how to lay a guilt trip on her father and she succeeded. Didn't she realize how much I missed my daughters and grandchildren when we were in Florida? It was her mother who relished the time away, not her father. I struggled with the issue every year.

This was exactly why I had decided not to tell the girls about my sexual identity crisis! Maybe she'd never be able to handle it. Then what would I do? I put the though aside. There was nothing I could do until we returned in March. And there was still no reply from my work friend. I feared the worst…but I still held out hope.

The next morning we invited our children and their families to a final brunch before we left. I wondered if this would be the last meal we would share together.

If he had lived, my father would be eighty-three years old next week—Groundhog's Day. I tried to imagine what he would think of me. He probably wouldn't be too surprised. I was far from being like my father. He was a man's man as they say. I was not even close to following in my father's footsteps, even though I had already outlived him by almost twenty years. I knew I didn't measure up. I was glad he wasn't alive to see my 'coming out'. I knew he would never understand. I'd been reading books about gay men and how they coped and how they could improve their lives. Curiously what I'd read said that the men I would seek out would be a mixture of the good and bad qualities of my father. I knew this was true from my recent encounters. All of the men I'd been attracted to bore a child's remembrance of my father—all were of similar age—late twenties or early thirties. They all had good physical characteristics—well built, confident men. Only two men came close to my real age and honestly I did not find them attractive. The teacher, Dan and the engineer all fit my father's mold, or at least my perception and recollection of him. Two out of three had subsequently rebuffed me, as my father had done years before.

At this precise moment in my life, I felt so alone again.

"...But sometimes you cross the line and never can go back home..."

I went to bed alone while my wife slept in our bed with the two granddaughters. They looked so angelic and peaceful by her side.

Sometime during the night I awoke to my youngest granddaughter's coughing. I lay awake agonizing..."Don't tell me she's getting sick again?" She'd just spent five days in the hospital before Christmas with pneumonia. I began to stress. Picking up my CD player, I put on the Josh Groban CD again. Maybe this would block the coughing. A half hour later she was still coughing. It brought back memories of when my own two daughters were her age and sometimes got sick. I was just listening to the song, "Broken Vow" when my emotions kicked in as I heard Josh sing—

> *I let you go*
> *I let you fly*
> *Now that I know, I'm asking why*
> *I let you go*
> *Now that I found*
> *A way to keep somehow*
> *More than a broken vow*

The tears flowed. I had fooled myself into thinking I was over Chris. When? Where was the one man who could help me navigate to pure joy? A man who wouldn't reject me? Giant steps forward, now a few steps back. Predictable I guess…

Sunday brunch came and went. I had to admit it was nice having everyone together. The grandkids were great! The baby slept in his chair the whole time, covered by the new 'boy' blanket I purchased in the hospital the day he was born. I could tell my daughter was distressed over our pending absence. Several times she brought up possible scenarios and how she could join us in Florida. After brunch, we said our goodbyes to the youngest and her family and followed our other daughter to her home to return some things. On the way there my wife mentioned the possibility of leaving for Florida sooner as ice and snow were forecast for the next day. After saying goodbyes again, we set out for home to pack the car and leave immediately.

When we reached home there were two phone messages. One was from my daughter; the other was from my work buddy. I was relieved to get the latter message, but reluctant to return his call. What would he say to me? What would I say to him? I dialed the number. Damn. Busy. I went to pack finally. I tried to call again. My friend's wife answered. She was seven months pregnant with her second child, a boy. She had a difficult pregnancy at first denying it even when the ultrasound confirmed it. She wasn't having an easy time emotionally. Her nine year old daughter wasn't handling her mother's pregnancy very well either.

I said the expected, "Hi how are you doing? Is xxx there?" My friend took the line followed by the exchange of pleasantries. Finally I asked if he had received my lengthy email. No. No wonder he was still pleasant; he didn't know the letter's content. After encouraging him to read it, I said goodbye and asked him to email me after he read the letter. I hoped he would, but that wasn't my decision. It rested with my friend.

As we pulled out of the driveway I was relieved. We were finally heading south. Our daughters would cope as best they could. Work was not an issue. Seven weeks away from this place, the available computer, chat lines, hook ups and rejections…

THE LONG AND WINDING ROAD SOUTH

My wife had been right about the weather. Two hours into our trip the snow started. After four hours it got worse; the roads deteriorated. I made the decision to stop for the night when they began to predict freezing rain. We got off the Interstate and checked into a motel.

Sometime during the night I began dreaming about my wife and I in Hawaii. We had been there twice before. This time we were again having a good time. No children with us on this trip. As I awoke the memory of the dream was still fresh in my mind. Taking a clue from my counselor I tried to analyze it. Either Chris had died or was near death. Chris and I had talked about going to Hawaii some day. When I believed Chris was dying, I asked Michael to remind Chris about Hawaii. Michael had used the money I sent to buy Chris the Hawaiian bouquet for the hospital.

Was this the long awaited sign from Chris? Was this Chris' way of telling me to stick with my wife and get on with the rest of our lives? I wanted desperately to believe this was the case. As for Chris' passing I wouldn't know until I got to Florida and checked for an email from Michael.

We had breakfast, scraped the ice of the car, repacked and set out again I read the paper while my wife drove. I pulled out my 'novel' and started to write down what I remembered about the dream. I'd have to tell my counselor about it. In my mind, I hoped again that Chris' journey had begun and Michael could begin his real grieving...

I had an enlightened revelation as we drove. I had always told people that the problem with my mother was that she always needed someone. I'd said the same thing about my youngest daughter. I realized that I needed other guys more than they likely needed me. The need was driving me, not the personal satisfaction of the moment. My aim was to please a man in order to feel needed. After meeting them, I would become their protectors. I acted paternal. I wanted a father-son emotional bond. I treated my youngest son-in-law in such a manner. I treated Chris and Michael that way. My last meet, Dan fit the same process. Even at work I acted that way—co-workers needed something; all they had to do was ask. No money for the vending machines no problem. Need money to feed your kids? No problem. It was the same with my grandchildren. When my girls were growing up I'd done the same with them. That's what this part of the journey was all about…being the father to any and all who were prepared to let me. I needed that bond and deeply felt rejection when it was broken. I always felt that if I hadn't come on so strong, some of the guys would still want to see me. I subverted my own joy in order to please them…

The fog was lifting as we left Louisville, Kentucky. The sun was peeping through. The roads on our journey were now clear. Was my fog lifting too? Were my roads clear as well?

At nightfall we stopped at another motel in Alabama. There was no snow or ice. We had finally left winter behind. The bleak emotional winter of the last six months would leave an impression which, unlike my granddaughters' snow angels would not disappear in the warmth of Florida.

We set out on the final leg of our journey the next morning. It would take about four more hours. I was anxious to get there to check my email. I hoped that, at least, there'd be a reply from my work buddy. That was not to be the case that afternoon, or even the following afternoon. I quickly emailed my friend, the teacher and Michael letting them know that I'd arrived safely, hoping to elicit a reply. I went to bed listening to the familiar sounds of Josh Groban. Ahead were six long weeks with my wife, her sister and at various times their brothers. "Que sera, que sera" as the song went.

We went shopping in the afternoon as was our usual activity in Florida. I found a really good deal on shoes which I couldn't resist. We went back to my brother-in-law's home and my wife did some washing. Later we went to a local coffee shop where I was able to email my counselor. Before dinner my brother-in-law and I went to the golf club to use the hot tub. I anticipated questions about my current health but they never came up, thankfully.

After the dinner I prepared we watched TV. When the programmes concluded, I got ready for bed. My wife joined me. What followed was tender lovemaking, which eventually became intense petting, kissing and fondling. At one point I asked my wife to stop stroking me for fear I would reach orgasm. Both of us rolled over and fell asleep. I couldn't engage in intercourse on this occasion, no matter how much I wanted to, the necessary condoms were not in my possession. I knew we were both disappointed.

This was a situation which had previously occurred between us. It always confused me. Romantically I still loved my wife and wanted sex with her. I always enjoyed it and felt she did too. I had read somewhere recently that gay men could still be romantically involved with a woman, but still be attracted physically to men. It was sex on a different plane.

I seemed to fit that description. The next day, while shopping, I made sure that I purchased some condoms so I would be prepared for our next encounter. I wanted it. For the next five days we would be visiting my other brother-in-law near West Palm Beach. I rubbed my finger across the coin I purchased at a pecan farm in Alabama. One side was inscribed with the Serenity Prayer; the other side read "One Day at a Time". Not a bad credo…

Three days since leaving home I had still not heard from my work buddy or Michael. I was anxious to hear from them, but it was not yet to be. We set out on the Friday for a side trip to St. Augustine, before heading to West Palm.

As we headed across Florida in the rain listening to Rod Stewart, my mind wandered once again to Michael and my friend. Right now these were the only two men who mattered—Michael for his connection to Chris, and my friend because he was my closest local friend. No word from either on email. I wouldn't be able to check again until we got to West Palm the next evening.

I would truly feel the loss of my friend's acquaintance if he turned on me. We first met while working in departments in the store. My friend was younger than I by eighteen years. Short in stature, like myself, we eventually came to work in the same department abut two years ago. We hit it off quickly. Both of us had the same work ethic which bonded us against the less ambitious people. When we weren't really busy our conversations turned to our personal lives. He was in a second marriage with a woman ten years younger. Life had not been easy. Her child was difficult for him to deal with. He was a no-nonsense stepfather. They had briefly separated but gotten back together only to learn that she was pregnant. His stepdaughter acted a lot like my granddaughter. The challenges of raising children whose fathers were still around brought us together. Each of us would relate his experiences to the other when no customers were around. As our friendship grew we went out to lunch when our schedules coincided. I had been to his house once to help him put a roof on a shed. In some sense, he was a surrogate son. Yet, when we were together the years between us were erased.

Prior to my hospitalization, I had begun to tell my friend of my difficulties at home. He knew only that my marriage was strained. When I was in the hospital, my friend called my wife inquiring about me. He was the only person from work to whom I would speak in the hospital. I felt that he would always be there for me. Lately, he had taken a different job in the company and I had been transferred to a different department. My friend worked the five a.m. shift, so if we met it was usually for breakfast, which was his lunch. Before I left for Florida I had been stymied in trying *to out myself to him. Now it would appear those meetings, and likely the friendship were things of the past. I was batting zero in maintaining real friends!*

FAMILY MATTERS

We spent the afternoon in St. Augustine doing the touristy things—riding the trolley for a tour of America's oldest city. There was so much to see; we couldn't possibly see it all in one afternoon. After dinner we shopped again, and then returned before going to bed. Early the next morning we would be heading south to West Palm, at which time I would once again have access to my email account. Would there be a reply from my friend or Michael?

We made our way to my other brother-in-law's home. They actually lived about twenty-eight miles from West Palm. The resort catered to seniors, many of them snowbirds from Canada. His home was situated on one of the many side streets with a golf-related name. It was a lovely Florida style home complete with hot tub. After the long ride this was very appealing. Before dinner, I logged on using the computer—no email messages. I quickly sent a note to Michael asking him to make a decision—continue to email me or tell me to get lost. I'd had enough of Michael's game of email torture. As for my friend, I wasn't quite ready to write him off.

After dinner we all sat outside relaxing over drinks. At some point in the conversation I asked my brother-in-law about a mutual friend with whom I'd worked. He had left teaching with what everyone thought was a nervous breakdown. I was shocked when I was told that it wasn't a nervous breakdown; the guy had outed himself after twenty-seven years of marriage! My wife and I were suddenly silent. I knew what she was thinking. Little did the others know what was on our minds? What would they think if they knew that I was gay? I wasn't about to tell them now, not here, probably not ever…

We eventually got into the hot tub and headed for bed around ten o'clock. My wife was very quiet. I was pensive after the earlier conversation. I didn't sleep very well, tossing and turning with a variety of dreams which left me unsettled. When I finally got out of bed, my wife was already up reading the newspaper. We both had something to eat and got dressed for the day. I was sitting on the porch when my wife went outside. She was going for a walk—without even asking me. I was hurt that she hadn't asked me. When she returned I was cool to her. She sensed it right away. What was wrong? Nothing…why couldn't I tell her I was hurt that she hadn't asked me on the walk? The tension passed when my brother-in-law asked us all to go for a walk to see the local clubhouse.

Next day was Super Bowl Sunday. We shopped and came home for dinner. While the others watched the game, my wife and I took a walk after dark. Upon returning I was able to log on to the computer. Eureka…a message from Michael! I quickly replied. As I was getting ready to send my message, Michael IM'd me. For the next half hour we chatted about Michael's classes, his girlfriend and his anger with Chris over the whole business of lying to me. Ironically I said the same things to Michael that Chris had said to me months back. Michael was so desperate for an end to the whole sorry saga. Sensing his despair, I sent him a cyber hug. Michael was thankful. It was obvious he had few shoulders to cry on in North Carolina, with the exception of his girlfriend. I asked Michael if she knew about me and was told she didn't. Just one more secret for Michael to keep. That wasn't fair. I had told Michael there would be no more lies; Michael now knew my real name. He asked if I would start calling him a pet name his friends used. I was pleased he now counted me as a friend. With my work buddy ignoring me, at least I had Michael to talk with, even if it was email. Michael was there for me when it appeared no one else was, with the exception of my wife.

I got through the next day alright. My wife and I went in to West Palm Beach and did some sightseeing and shopping. When we returned my wife's other brother and his wife were there from the north. After an enjoyable dinner we headed out towards the hot tub, but before that we just sat around and talked At some point the conversation connected to the restaurant "Hooters" notorious for its' scantily clad waitresses. I brought up the discrimination lawsuit brought against them by some male waiters. My younger brother-in-law jumped in with something like "You sure as hell wouldn't find any queers there, why would a man want to work there?" Like many comments over the last few months, the inference to queers or gays stung. I was still so sensitive and probably always would be. I was starting to realize what the guys in group counseling had told me about attitudes towards gays in general. My skin wasn't yet thick enough to rebuff the comments. If this is how my wife's family reacted to gays, what could I expect of my own daughters? I sat quietly in the hot tub contemplating my disclosure at the end of our stay in Florida.

The next day and evening went better for me. They were all celebrating the younger brother's sixty-fourth birthday with a steak dinner. After we returned to the porch to talk and read. First the women and then the men used the hot tub. When we were all done, all except my wife's sister and I went inside. We sat outside and talked—pleasantries at first and then more serious. It led to a discussion of psychia-

trists and counselors. Without divulging my secret I started to talk about my counseling sessions and how much they were helping me. I felt like telling her the truth right there and then, but declined just as I had earlier when we were all together, even though my mind played out several scenarios. Now wasn't the time; my children had to be told first. In-laws would have to wait. I turned in for the night after several glasses of wine. Tomorrow we were heading back up north to the Panhandle—a seven hour trip. Once again I'd be able to check my email for news from my work buddy and Michael.

JUST THE TWO OF US

I sat alone in the spa at our condo. There had been no news from Michael, but there was a message from Jack. Up until this time I hadn't written anything about Jack in my journal. I wasn't quite sure why. I had met Jack online before I went into the hospital and we had gone for the preliminary coffee near Jack's apartment. Jack wasn't like the other guys. In fact, he was more like me—middle aged, slightly overweight—just the opposite of the other men. He was a quiet man, well educated and had been married before he came out. He had children who were aware of his sexual preferences. Until recently, Jack had a live-in partner, but he had been transferred out of the city.

I wasn't attracted to Jack physically, but Jack was a good listener. After our first meeting I was reluctant to meet him again. When I was aware that Jack had logged on the chat line, I logged off. Having ignored him for over a month, I finally relented and agreed on a second meeting. I realized that Jack was much more experienced than me, judging by our conversation that night (as well as his actions). I wasn't comfortable with the direction our discussion went.

After this meeting I didn't see Jack for some time. We continued to talk online. Jack was like a counselor to me at this time. I told Jack all that was going through my mind and he was supportive. This led to a third meeting after Christmas. We started with a long discussion about coming out and the emotional costs, drank a little wine and ended up satisfying each others needs once again.

When I'd arrived in Florida, Jack had sent me an email wishing me a good time. I had responded something about missing his company. In a subsequent email I sought Jack's advice on being rejected by the guys I had grown fond of. Jack's response was measured. I'd felt strange asking Jack about this, after all I was rejecting Jack for the others, at least in my mind. Jack was becoming more of a friend…a good friend and I told him how much I appreciated it.

As I sat in the spa my thoughts turned to Jack's advice. Did I want a relationship or just a playmate? As long as I was married, no other guy would likely enter into a relationship…there was no future. On the other hand, playmates were attainable—even married ones.

I was feeling confused again. I wished I could talk with my counselor. He had told me that some guys still maintained a relationship with women. I was thinking I might not be able to do that much longer. I went inside, dried off, dressed and made myself a drink.

Dear Dad,

Well it's been three months since I last wrote you. If you'd been watching you're probably very disappointed in me. They tell me that being gay is not environmental; it just happens that way for some unknown reason. I am also told that I was 'wired' that way from birth.

In undergoing counseling I have been trying to come to terms with my past, the past you were briefly a part of. What I have come to realize is, although you didn't make me age, you set in motion my desire to please other men, because I wasn't able to please you in life. The men I have sought out are you!—Same age, same body type, etc. When I am with them, I feel like the younger person. I try very hard to please them in the only way I know how to right now.

I have come to accept that this makes me gay even though I love my wife and family. I have disappointed my wife, yet she stands by me at this point. She is the only person who has done so consistently, so I know she truly loves me and isn't about to reject me like all the men in my life have up to this point. I can't begin to imagine what she is feeling inside, aside from the hurt and anger, and likely shame. I don't know how long she can continue bearing the burden of me. In this way we are probably like mother and you.

I probably won't write you again. There's no further need for me to tell you how I am feeling. Someday it will all be in print. I'm writing a novel to document my 'journey'. I've tentatively dedicated it to the men in my life, starting with you. What do you think of the title—"Not My Father's Footsteps"? I think that says it all...bye now...hope someday you'll understand...

I finished my letter and headed off to bed, hoping for a good night's sleep. There was still one month's vacation ahead.

Half way through the next day I realized I had forgotten to take my medications. Since the hospital I had been on two anti-depressants to help me relieve my anxieties.

It was too late now. I had gone over to my brother-in-law's house in the pouring Florida rains to catch up on my email and do a load of washing. My 'journal' was with me. I had decided I would re-read it all and make a decision about allowing my wife to read my tell-all story.

I logged on to the computer and saw a message from Jack. He was cautioning me against telling workplace friends, as I had done with my friend. He suggested some mental exercises to help me cope with my current dilemma. I responded to Jack thanking him once again for being there for me. It seemed no one else was, aside from my wife.

Returning to the condo I decided she should read all that I had written. While it was a truthful attempt to document my journey, I had purposefully left out the obvious sexual details and names, which could be too much information for anyone, other than me and my conscious.

After dinner we headed for the spa, with me remaining after my wife went inside. I knew she would be reading my journal. As I sat alone, looking for stars in the cloudy night sky, I was overwhelmed with emotion. Symbolic—me sitting in a large tub of hot water alone. I couldn't fool myself, I still missed Chris. Maybe if Chris could be told I was still here for him it would help him overcome this terminal illness. Although not a religious person, I asked God to let Chris know I was still waiting for him. I knew that if I sent Chris a message via Michael it would not reach him, as Michael hadn't seen Chris since before Christmas. I couldn't contact Chris' parents. Who was this? How did I know their son? Michael had warned me not to do this. He was right. The jets shut down on the spa and I went inside.

My wife was reading my journal. As I entered the bedroom she briefly looked up without speaking. I dried off and lay on the bed watching some inane programme while I fretted about what she was reading and thinking. It took her a couple of hours to get through the one hundred and forty plus pages. When she finished she put it aside and left the room. Not a good sign. I lay there waiting for her to return which she eventually did, carrying two glasses of wine left over from dinner. Finally I asked if she had any questions,. We talked for a while about my journey and how I was doing. Sometimes I felt the tears welling up inside. She was very perceptive of my fragile nature at the moment. She hugged me and held me lovingly.

We both returned to watching TV—some Mel Gibson flick. I longed to hold her again. I was lucky to have her all these years. I thought the opposite must be her reality now. She certainly wouldn't consider herself lucky in this situation. As we held each other we became more intimate. I needed her so badly—the only person who had ever really loved me!

I thought the sex was mutually satisfying, in spite of stopping in the middle to utilize the required condom, which was now part of our routine. We held each other tightly afterwards.

I wondered about what had occurred. How in hell could I so thoroughly enjoy sex with her and still be gay? Maybe I wasn't really gay…yeah right!

I slept fairly well, having at least taken my two nightly sleep inducers. I remembered no dreams. When I awoke it was straight to the spa—my daily routine. I was soon joined by my wife. The weather was finally co-operating. When the jets stopped this time, we got out and went to get dressed for the day. I briefly read the morning paper. We intended on going to the local coffee shop for coffee and tea and to read more newspapers.

The shop had Internet access, so I was able to access my email account. When I logged on, my heart momentarily stopped. There was a message from my work buddy. Quickly opening the message I read solemnly. My friend had suspected I might be gay all along, as apparently had others at work. And, no, he could not continue being my friend. I wished him well and told him we could still be amicable at work—no more lunches or breakfasts. My friend wanted no part of that. He couldn't condone the lifestyle of his now former buddy.

I sent a short reply to his message, respecting his decision, but regretting the end of our friendship. I finally had the answer I had waited two weeks for. My counselor was right; I wasn't really surprised, but then again, someone I once felt close to was now gone—not dead, but gone nonetheless. The cost of coming out just got a bit higher.

As I sat alone in the spa the next evening, I looked up again at the stars. The sky was clear; the stars blanketed all above me, unlike the previous night. In the western sky one star in particular stood out. I didn't know whether it was Venus or whatever. It was big and shiny. As I sat submerged in the 100 degree water I asked God to carry that star to Chris once again with the message to let go. It had now been over three months since Chris was hospitalized. His prognosis was bleak. Why was he holding on? Perhaps he too held out hope for our eventual reunion. Maybe he was giving Michael time to prepare himself emotionally. Or just maybe he was waiting to make sure I found another true friend to be my soul mate, as Chris had been.

I wanted Chris to pass peacefully. My most recent rejection by my work buddy led me to believe there wasn't likely anyone else for me to call a friend. I could only hope to join Chris soon, but in keeping with my promise, it would never be by my own hand. Why was God keeping me here?

Dear Chris;

Well it's been several weeks since I wished you a safe and speedy passage from your earthly pains. I am trying hard to move on like you wanted me to, but while you are still alive I can't give up hope for you and your family and friends, especially Michael. I don't know much about your family, other than what I saw on your web page, but I have come to know Michael. He tells me he feels guilty when I chat with him in light of the pretense of your death in November. He is hurting very badly. I try to get him to talk about you but he's still a little angry with you for making him lie to me. I've told him time and again that what happened these last three months was history. Put it aside. He's not quite ready. He's angry and depressed, much like I was when he told me you were still alive.

I want so much to be able to talk with you again—to let you know I'm still here for you, but Michael feels that wouldn't be a good idea, as your parents know nothing of our relationship (I think). Sending you a card would not be appropriate either, I guess.

Since Michael hasn't spoken to you recently, I haven't been able to tell you about my continued vigil. It's not that I haven't been after him to do so!

Hopefully you've heard the messages I keep sending via the stars at night. I can't help missing you...

Fate brought you into my life at a time when I was at the bottom. You rekindled my spirit, but at the same time, caused me to rethink the direction of my life. I questioned. You questioned. Together we were working through our own personal demons.

You encouraged me to be strong as I moved out of the past. In some way, I hope I gave you hope for the future, albeit temporary. Am I still giving you hope? I want to believe that so badly!

I miss our evenings on the computer, sharing thoughts and feelings.

I miss the sound of your laughter when we spoke on the telephone.

I miss your words of wisdom (even when I didn't believe them).

I miss the person you are, caring, sensitive, yet supportive.

I miss the holidays we never shared. I miss what might have been, but probably wouldn't have been.

Realistically we would probably never have met face to face. Were we fooling ourselves all along? Maybe I read too much into things. Maybe I was too desperate. I'm not sorry you came into my life. I will always be grateful for our brief relationship. You have impacted me in ways you would never have imagined.

Please forgive me my indiscretions, my unfaithfulness these last three months. You opened doors for me that had been closed for almost forty years.

Thank you, my dear Chris.

No matter how hard I try, your influence on me lives on. That is your legacy to me. I will always love you!

Love Bryan

LIFE WITH JACK

I was missing Jack; there was no doubt about it. Our daily emails were something I looked forward to. Jack was someone I could be honest with, but it was too soon to say whether Jack would play any long enduring role in my life. I wasn't sure at this point that I wanted him to. Jack was 'Mr. Right Now' as a woman might say.

Sitting in the spa, I was struck by the imagery of the moment. Here I was again sitting in a kettle of bubbling liquid. The bubbles represented my wife, my daughters, our friends, my work and the men in my life. I was surrounded on all sides. Up to my neck in hot water...

My wife came down and joined me. We sat there in silence. No doubt she was thinking about our situation. I was too. I knew we needed to start the off-put marriage counseling as soon as we returned to Canada. I knew all of the past months were so unfair to her. I couldn't yet comprehend why she remained so tolerant. Maybe she thought this phase would pass. Or maybe she was hanging on for the kids. Just maybe she didn't know how to end the marriage without losing face. All were concerns which I had as well, yet we hadn't discussed any of them. My current counselor was very good at helping me deal with my life, especially the past. My wife didn't yet have a counselor. What we needed was a counselor/mediator to get us talking openly about our future—together or apart. There was so much left up in the air. No doubt we were getting by one day at a time. We still had twenty-six days before leaving Florida. Those days would pass quickly and then there would be many necessary animated discussions.

For the next several days I received email only from Jack who was still in Toronto on business. He would be back at home on the Friday and then perhaps I could actually telephone him. I hadn't heard from Michael and as the days went by, I became anxious to hear from him.

Saturday evening came, Valentine's Day. We attended a dinner party at her brother's place along with some of their friends. We bade our goodbyes about nine o'clock and headed back to the condo. For the next three hours I worked on a jigsaw puzzle I had purchased to pass the rainy days—four this week alone!

When I finally went to be at one o'clock I knew I wasn't going to sleep. Shutting off the TV I lay there awake in the darkened room while my wife slept beside me. Obliv-

ious to my sleeplessness. My mind wandered to Chris, Michael and Jack. Without hearing from Michael I had no word of Chris. Perhaps he had died and Michael couldn't tell me. Maybe something happened to Michael himself. He was despondent the last time we spoke. I had given him my phone number in Florida and I had sent him some phone card numbers so he wouldn't have to pay the long distance, if he needed to call me for any reason.

After an hour or so of mental gymnastics, I decided to put on my headset and listen to some Josh Groban. This always brought me some small piece of mind, but it also washed over me with memories. When next I looked at the bedside clock it was three forty-five in the morning! Still awake, I shut off the CD player and rolled over to sleep. When I awoke it was six forty-five after endless dreams, which always left me confused when I tried to interpret them.

I got up and headed to the spa to start my day. We were now halfway through our stay in Florida. After breakfast I headed to the Internet café to check my email—still only Jack—now home. I replied then proceeded to send a quick note to Michael. While I was at it I emailed my counselor back home, updating him on how things were going.

When I returned to the condo my wife was sitting upstairs reading the latest of my writings. There followed a brief discussion of what I had put down. She still couldn't comprehend my uneasiness with her calm demeanor. I tried to explain that were I in her shoes I'd feel very different. She assured me she was here for the long haul.

How can you spend three weeks with your best friend and still feel alone? She was indeed my best friend for better or worse, in sickness and in health. She had been there through our youngest daughter's challenging adolescent years. I had been there for her when first her parents died and then her sister. She was there when my career changed directions and I became involved in various community organizations. She was more than willing to look after my aging mother with whom I was never comfortable. It was she who managed my mother's finances and arranged for housekeepers, manicures and haircuts. She always remembered to phone my mother when I didn't want to.

She was a great wife and mother. She was totally supportive of everything I did. She was a caring person to family and friends. While working full-time she completed her university degree. I became the chief cook and financial officer in the marriage. She cleaned house, took an active role in managing our household and kept everyone clean and well-dressed.

I never ever doubted she loved both me and our children and grandchildren. She was generous in time and material things for the girls and their families. Together we made sure all were well cared for. We saw one or more of our grandchildren every week day. She made it a point to talk with each of the girls daily.

After we retired we both had gone to work part-time. We loved traveling and did so often. When our girls were younger we traveled as a family almost always. It wasn't until near retirement when we started to travel by ourselves. Even then, we would often include her/our best friend whose husband had died the week before her own sister. Occasionally she and her girlfriends would go off for long weekends of shopping. I never disallowed her, in fact, I encouraged her to go and have fun.

We shared a love for theatre and had seen numerous Broadway plays either in Toronto or Detroit. Sometimes we went to movies, but she really didn't like sitting still that long; she always had to be busy. At home she went from one task to another all day long. When we retired she took over our financial affairs; I had done it all our working lives. Unlike me, she was a better money manager. As much as she disliked it she did better than I had. She took care of herself, taking pride in her appearance. She had regular hair appointments and manicures and looked younger than her near-sixty years when I had dropped the bombshell.

She was indeed my best friend; she was a female friend. I'd never had any real male friends after adolescence. This was what I had always been lonely for.

My wife and I headed for the spa after dinner. It was a beautiful Florida night—the stars shone bright overhead. I was pensive as always. She asked what I had been writing about—I said, "Loneliness". When we were sitting there I mentioned that I had not heard from Michael for well over a week. I felt that probably indicated Chris was gone. She indicated agreement with my thinking. I'd heard daily from Jack. That was always good. I'd tried calling him to no avail. He was either out of town or at Church doing work. I wanted to hear his voice. I needed to hear his voice. Tomorrow I was going fishing on the Gulf of Mexico with my brother-in-law. The next day we were day tripping to Biloxi, Mississippi on a gambling trip (not that we ever had been serious gamblers—just nickel and quarter slots, even in Las Vegas). I wouldn't hear from Jack on either day.

When we left the spa we went to our bedroom to change out of our wet swimsuits. I thought long and hard and finally, hesitantly, I asked my wife if she minded me making a phone call to Jack. Much to my relief she replied, "No", and added "Don't ever ask again". I wasn't offended. She was saying there was no reason to ask her permission. I let her know I was being sensitive to her feelings. This was one trait of mine that was constant. I always worried about how everyone else felt. To this end I always submerged my own.

I dialed Jack's number and waited to hear his voice. Please be there...On the third ring he answered. It was so good to hear his voice again. We kept the conversation on *a casual level, discussing Jack's weight loss, the weather, Jack's trip to Toronto. Jack was keeping busy with work. He'd visited his son in Michigan on the weekend. He was headed out of town on business the first week of March. He'd be back in town shortly after we returned from Florida. Too soon the conversation ended, but I felt better having talked to him for the first time in three weeks.*

The only thing on my mind as I went to bed that evening was tomorrow's fishing trip…seven hours on a small fishing boat in the Gulf of Mexico…

I slept fitfully that night worried that I would oversleep. This was my usual habit when I had to wake early for an event. I didn't trust alarm clocks. When I was younger, I had no problem getting up for work. I awoke finally at six a.m. and got ready for the fishing trip. Our boat was called Sweet Jody…seven hours surrounded by smelly bait and water everywhere. Oh well, it was an adventure! Seven hours and one fish later we returned to the dock…no fish dinner tonight! Burgers and salad would be on the menu. My wife met us on the dock, camera in hand waiting for the picture of me and my catch…yes, right. She so loved taking pictures.

On the way home I stopped at the Internet café and once again checked my email—two from Jack, one from my youngest daughter. As always Jack was there with his words of wisdom.

"Don't take rejection so hard—there are many reasons why men don't return your messages. A lot of men are only looking for playmates and never would commit so soon to one person. Take it easy. Mediate. Consider some spiritual help. Keep seeing your counselor. Stop over thinking the situation"

As always…sensible words. Jack had been out for over seven years now and was trying hard to keep me balanced. No matter what happened in the future, I knew I could talk to Jack like no one else.

Early the next morning we headed to Biloxi by bus. We sat side by side, mostly in silence. This was our usual pattern when we traveled. I had brought along my CD player and my usual Josh Groban CD. As we passed along the interstate, Florida, Alabama and Mississippi, I thought for a moment of being on the bus alone, heading I didn't know where—leaving behind everyone and everything I had known in life. The thought overwhelmed me and I became teary-eyed. I knew I had nowhere to go, nor was I ready, and I still wasn't sure that was what I wanted. I had thought our time away from home would help me reach some decisions on my future and our future. I was still no further ahead, and our time in Florida was about over. Once our children knew the truth about me I might be forced to make that decision. Tomorrow was another day...

The first time we had sex was our wedding night. After the reception we'd gone to our new apartment. As teachers we didn't have much money, school started ten days after our marriage. There was neither time nor money for a honeymoon.

I recalled she was wearing a white cotton eyelet nightgown with matching peignoir. What I was wearing I couldn't recall—I usually slept in the nude since marriage, but likely had on pajama bottoms that night.

As we lay in bed hugging and kissing I thought I'd said something like "Shall we?" and we stumbled through sexual intercourse for the first time. I had read some books; I wasn't sure where her sexual information came from—probably her younger, married sister. We were both pretty awkward this first time. We probably should have used some lubricant but had none—too shy to buy it probably. I remembered in the morning I felt rather sore from the thrusting and rubbing.

We never talked about sex much. For the first few years it was missionary style. As we grew more comfortable other positions were experimented with. We fondled each other but oral sex was never a consideration. She took birth control bills, until after the birth of our second child, when I had a vasectomy. Sex was a regular part of our lives and both enjoyed it. Neither ever said much during or after sex. In the beginning we were both shy discussing this detail of our lives. In the last few years, the sex had become more relaxed and more adventuresome, but we still never discussed it much, even though it was my wife who would frequently ask what she might do for me to make it more enjoyable.

After the casino trip we went to bed. My wife had sensed my moodiness and moved across the king sized bed to hug me. I reciprocated. She proceeded to rub my back and when I turned over she began rubbing my chest, working her way down my body. I was fully aroused by then and she continued to make sure I stayed that way. After a few minutes I undid her pajama top and began caressing her breasts. I eventually began kissing her deeply, which she always seemed to enjoy. I rubbed my hands over her naked body. She felt so warm. I pressed myself into her abdomen while the kissing continued.

When I stopped kissing her, my tongue gently moved down her body. What followed was some intense oral sex, which we had both come to enjoy in the last few years. When the time came for intercourse, she was on top, a position most women are supposed to like. The now ritual condom was in place. My full attention was on the moment.

As we lay there afterwards, I was confused. How could I so thoroughly enjoy sex with her yet still need a man? The sex was different with a man, but equally good. Why wasn't it enough?

I got up and went to the bathroom to clean up and brush my teeth. When I got back to bed, she went into the bathroom. I lay there contemplating what had just happened between us. Besides the confusion, I felt saddened, which she sensed when she came back into bed. She apologized for making me feel that way. I didn't respond immediately and felt ashamed by my lack of response. It wasn't her fault I felt this way; she'd done everything she could to make me happy. I started to sob quietly while reaching out to grab her shoulder—my way of trying to let her know it wasn't her fault I guess. The tears continued for awhile, after which I turned over and fell asleep.

I couldn't help but thinking, because we were each other's best friend, neither could ever imagine being apart, but being together was not getting any easier.

I checked my email the next day. The only mail was from Jack. I was starting to realize that Michael was history. I understood Michael's withdrawal. I'd sent a couple of brief emails to the teacher and Dan, again with no responses. Right now, Jack was all I had and I was thankful, even though Jack was still 2500 km away in Canada. It wouldn't be much longer. I'd told Jack about my wife's suggestion about getting away. We agreed to discuss it when I got home. There was a lot about Jack that I didn't know and vice versa. Maybe we wouldn't be compatible in the long run. Jack just might end up being Mr. Right Now. We both needed much more time. I didn't want to get hurt, as I had over Chris, nor did I want to presume about Jack's true feelings. Indeed, we needed to talk more.

Saturday was the best weather day yet. It was sixty-five degrees and sunny when we awoke and quickly climbed into the low seventies. After a short stay in the spa, I had breakfast, read the paper and headed to the Internet café. I knew there was a message from Jack, as we had spoken on the telephone the evening before. I felt good hearing his voice and not just seeing words on a computer screen. Jack warned me not to be upset when I read his message. I knew that Jack was heading to Chicago for a few days in early March. Jack had previously indicated that he might be going back to school, changing careers. I had suspected that it would be not in Windsor. My suspicions were confirmed. Jack was planning on going back to school, not in Windsor, but Chicago. The course he was taking would mean he'd be away from Windsor for the next two years! He'd only be in Windsor on holidays and during any breaks in his schedule.

I took it fairly well. Everything was unconfirmed until after Jack came back from there. Maybe he wouldn't be accepted. Selfishly I hoped that might be the case. Morally, if that was what Jack wanted then I had no business standing in his way. Who was I at this moment? Jack and I were nowhere near being partners…One day at a time…if Jack did leave it wouldn't be until early summer. Right now that seemed a long way off…

Jack's email expressed interest in the two of us going away for a few days when I returned. At least he was still interested in exploring our relationship more—no doors were yet closed. My wife had suggested getting away when I got home. I presumed she didn't expect me to go alone. After I told the children about being a gay man would likely be a good time to do this. It would give my wife some time alone to explore her feelings as well. I responded to Jack's email with more questions apologizing for making him a sounding board for my random thoughts. Who else could I ask?

Before leaving the café I wrote one more brief letter to Michael in North Carolina. Almost two weeks had passed with no word, no response. Today I would say goodbye to Chris' best friend. I promised not to contact him ever again, at the same time assuring him that he could email or telephone me anytime or anywhere. I owed that much to Chris—be there for Michael! I wished him well in his future, ending my email with the anticipation that this chapter in my life was over. Chris had helped me to open the doors of my emotional closet. The rest was up to me and me alone.

I lay there that night rehashing my discussion with Jack and wondering about Michael. In all honesty I'd never get Michael or Chris out of my psyche. As for Jack, I wondered why I'd had such feelings when we still barely new each other. Was I grasping for a safe place…a haven? What was it about Jack that comforted me?

When we got home from Florida, my wife and I would look closely over our finances, perhaps involving our financial planner. We still had a substantial mortgage and bills. I'd allowed her to take control of our finances for the last several years. I needed to know where we were financially. The difficulty would be convincing my wife that we should see a lawyer. We each needed to know our rights outside the marriage. I knew she'd be resistant. I was doing this for her good. She had to be aware that she had options and rights too. This did not mean I felt the marriage was over! We had to be realistic. If we eventually separated we both would know the implications while we were still speaking amicably. I still was far from convinced we couldn't stay together while I indulged my sexual desires with men, but could she really live like that? The rest of our lives? It was too much to expect of anyone, let alone someone she had been faithful to for thirty-seven years.

What if she were having the affairs? How would I feel? I knew. After the initial anger and hurt I'd be questioning myself. What had I done wrong? What could I have done differently? Was I not attentive enough? Didn't I satisfy her sexually? These were no doubt the same questions she was asking herself now. I didn't think I could stand by knowing she was having an affair. I couldn't encourage such a relationship. The images in my mind of her with someone else had entered my mind on several occasions, back when we were still both working. My unstable mind thought she was too friendly with another male teacher. I dismissed it as nonsense! She would never do that. She probably had thought the same of me, at some point but I couldn't ever remember who she might have thought me too friendly with at work.

It would drive me crazy to be at work knowing she was with someone else, but that is what I forced her to do after that Sunday in November. No doubt every time she went to work now and I wasn't going, she wondered what I would be up to. Up until now I never went out when she was at home—I tried to be sensitive to her feelings. I felt guilty sneaking around. When Marco had suggested I meet him late at night when she was asleep, I always declined. At some point I'd have to be more open, but I couldn't imagine telling her that I was going out on a date with another guy while she sat home. It was still unfathomable…but it would eventually have to happen.

I went to the café the next morning looking for my daily message from Jack. To my surprise there was a message from Michael! He chided me for thinking he didn't want to talk to me any more. Michael had been ill for two weeks and hadn't bothered to check his email. He was now better and apologized for not responding sooner. As for Chris, Michael had seen his sister and was told there was no change. It had now been over three months since Chris entered the hospital. Michael didn't know why he was hanging on.

I responded thanking Michael for getting back to me. I'd been worried about his health—physical and mental and he seemed okay now. I inquired about his girlfriend Karen but otherwise kept my reply short as others were waiting for the computer. I reminded him about feeling free to call me, here or when back at home—with or without news of Chris. And finally, I asked Michael that if the opportunity arose, to let Chris know I still thought about him and cared about his well-being. In reality I knew Michael would not likely do that, but I had to ask.

With that done I turned to Jack's email. He'd had a good visit with his daughter and was looking forward to my return from Florida in two weeks. I kept my reply short, explaining that I would talk to him on the telephone later that evening. My last email was to my oldest daughter—directions for them getting to Florida on Thursday. They had decided to drive down—two daughters and four kids—two days in a van.

With that I shut down the computer. We finished our beverages and headed for breakfast. On the way there I was going to stop off and make copies of my 'journal' papers. We stopped at IHOP, had the pages copied at the next door UPS Store and headed out for some more shopping. It was raining again—what else to do? Finally my wife picked up the pages and started to read them again…

She made no mention of Jack's possible leaving the city—after all, it wasn't confirmed was it? She agreed about the financial planner, but was steadfast in her refusal to see a lawyer. What was the point? If we split up, it would be fifty-fifty. I couldn't convince her. I didn't pursue it any further. She made no comment about my going away for a weekend, maybe that would come later.

After shopping we headed back to the condo. As soon as we grabbed something to eat, she picked up my writings again. What followed was a discussion of our financial affairs, her reason for not wanting a lawyer and her desire that I needed to do what I needed to do once we returned home. I wanted to ask if that meant the trip with Jack, but held back. I told her how guilty I felt sneaking around on her; I was still reticent about being open about such meetings. I had to get over that.

Another rainy day followed. We planned a trip to the nearby library to use their computers for a longer period of time. I needed to make arrangements for taking my oldest granddaughter to Disney World when she arrived. Logging on, I had an email from Michael, but not Jack. I was disappointed. Michael had just come from the doctor's having been diagnosed with a sinus infection. He had spoken with Chris' mother. Chris was having good and bad days. There was no mention of getting a card or message to Chris, which I had earlier asked about. In reply I kept the dialogue light, but couldn't avoid commenting about Chris. I so desperately wanted Chris to know I was still here for him, but how? It was best for everyone except Chris that I not try to contact him. When Michael mentioned about Chris' mother talking to him by telephone, my heart skipped a beat. If only I could talk with Chris…

My email to Jack was rather lengthy too. I needed him to know how much I missed him. Only twelve more days and I'd be home, but Jack would be in Chicago until the Thursday after our return. I made plans to see him as soon as he got back to Windsor. It had been so long. Neither of us was very forthright in our email writings. What I wanted to say to Jack, I couldn't say on a computer screen. It just wasn't the same.

After the library we headed to a movie, Jack Nicholson and Diane Keaton. Nicholson was not one of my favourites. I watched but didn't get too involved. It wasn't that great. When it finally ended we went for a quick burger and stopped by Barnes and Noble so I could pick up the gay health book I had seen the previous night.

My knowledge of the issues was limited to what I had read about HIV, hepatitis and oral sex. There was so much I didn't know or fully understand. I needed information and answers as I headed further out of the closet. My wife was concerned about my physical safety. I wanted to be sure I was cognizant of all of the repercussions of my lifestyle choice before I got into any problems. I had thought my family doctor would not be a useful source of information after my last visit.

I was tired of being away from home…I was tired of being away from Jack. I started reading the medical book as soon as I got home. Written by a gay doctor, it was factual, easy to read and objective in its' discussions of HIV, hepatitis, oral and anal sex, and various sexually transmitted diseases. There were very few pictures, but it was clearly written. I could only assume that the doctor knew what he was talking about. He offered many cautionary notes about drugs and possible physical injuries that gay men and even straight men might incur. Before going to bed I had read the whole book! I knew I should re-read it to make sure that I had understood what I had read, but would do that again when I returned home, letting what I had read sink in.

Waking the next morning, I shaved, put on a swim suit and headed for the spa, where I was joined by my wife. We sat in the hot tub waking up our tired bodies. We dried off, took showers, had a bite to eat and dressed to go out for the day. First stop, as usual, the café. I had two messages, one from Jack, and one from the teacher. The latter was getting ready for March Break back home. He was inquiring whether I'd been able to find any adult video stores in Florida; he was looking for a couple of titles unavailable in Canada. In a short email I let him know I had been unsuccessful so far, but I would keep trying as we headed back up north.

Jack's email was in response to mine of the previous day. I had told him about my wife's refusal to consult a lawyer seeing no reason for such. Jack cautioned me that even though we might see a financial planner each should consult a lawyer early on. If we ever did separate each needed to be in a position of knowledge.

Before going out for dinner, I started reading my third book, "Outing yourself" by Michelangelo Signorile (1996) as I was reading, a light bulb went on in my head. All this time I thought I was out. I couldn't figure out why I was still so confused about my identity. My counselor never really brought it up. I was out to my wife, her girlfriend, my ex brother-in-law, my doctor and my friend at work. I was still not really out to myself!

I still hadn't fully accepted that I was truly gay. That's why I was confused with my sexual activities with my wife. Some people knew I was gay, but not my mother or my children. I needed to get past that. I felt rejected by the men I'd been with, instead of *seeing them as friends on the journey, part of my growth as a gay man. I'd cut them off. I needed to reconnect but on a different plain. I needed all of them in one way or another. I needed to get past my "self-loathing" of gays I found effeminate. I needed to get past the homophobia I had grown up with. I had to accept myself for what I really was—a gay man—a homo, a queer, a fag. That's what I was and always had been; I had to accept the evidence and learn to be proud of who I was, not what I was, but what I was now...*

I needed to complete my coming out when I returned, not just telling individuals, but working at overcoming self-loathing and homophobic attitudes.

In my group counseling I had to learn to accept the differences of my counseling partners. Accept the effeminate young man; accept the gay man with the chip on his shoulder, just as I had accepted the other two guys. Accept them for what they are...appreciate their differences, just as they appreciated me.

This thinking was significant. I needed to let my counselor know what I had discovered, let Jack know and lastly, let the significant men I had encountered in the last six months know how much I still valued their friendship even if we were no longer sexually involved. I needed them as friends with no strings attached. I needed to be able to at least talk with them. Tomorrow I would email Mark, Dan and Marco. I wanted them to know I needed them to continue with me on this path of discovery...

We had a great dinner out with our northern friends...too much wine (since we'd stopped drinking two weeks ago). When we got home we got a call from our daughters who were now halfway to Florida. We headed to the spa. At one point I notice my wife's eyes tearing up. I encouraged her to open up, let it out. She was feeling melancholy thinking this could be one of our last social outings as a couple...I patiently explained this didn't have to be the case. No matter what, there was no reason why we couldn't continue to socialize as a couple...friends getting together with friends. I hoped we could always be friends no matter what happened. We meant too much to each other to let it dissolve away. I reiterated that what was occurring was not her fault in any way.

I knew things were progressing. My ultimate goal was to be happy "in my own skin" before I died. Accepting myself as a gay man was crucial to the process, before moving forward. Tomorrow I would really begin the process...

At the library I did as planned, emailing Jack, my counselor and the guys I had previously identified—Marco. Mark, etc. It felt good connecting with them on this level. To each I indicated a desire to rekindle the friendships, if nothing more than to be sounding boards to each other in times of need. I wasn't looking for anything sexual from them.

Jack and I had talked a little about the weeks ahead, after he got back from Chicago. He still wasn't positive on being able to get time away depending on whether he headed off to school or stayed. I confirmed to Jack that I had visited the Church website, searching for some spiritual guidance. This was a new church in the city with a small inclusive base of people. It was affiliated with other churches internationally. Jack was a local member. As I reviewed the website I came across the five basic precepts—

1. ***God is all active in everything, anywhere.***
2. ***I am naturally good because God's Divinity is in me and everyone.***
3. ***I create my experiences by what I choose to think and what I feel and believe.***
4. ***Through affirmative prayer and meditation I connect with God and bring out the god in my life.***
5. ***I do and give my best by living the Truth I know. I make a difference.***

As I read through them, I quickly copied them down for later reflection.

I'd often asked myself "Why?" "Why did my father have to die so young?" "Why does Chris continue to suffer?" "Why was I gay?" Just maybe my time had come to reconnect. I had thought about it often since I was hospitalized in October, but was never sure how or where to go. When I had more time I'd explore the site and the Church further.

Before I left the computer I emailed my work friend. I wasn't retreating on what I had said prior to leaving the city, or in response to my friend's email telling me he was not prepared to continue our friendship. Rather I wanted him to know I could accept his rejection even though I didn't understand it. I let him know how much better I was finally doing. I concluded by wishing he and his wife well with the new baby. (I later found out, his son had already been born by this time and had experienced some difficulties at birth which were not life threatening).

COMPANY'S HERE

Later that afternoon our daughters and grandchildren arrived from Canada. I was really glad to see them all, especially my new grandson, who was only one week old when we left for Florida.

It didn't take long for me to change my mind. They'd had a long trip and both mothers and children had spent too much time together. The condo was quickly turned upside down with toys and kids, but I tried to keep my cool. After dinner I was anxious for everyone to just go to bed! How quickly the old stressful feelings came back. When they were home and both families came to dinner I also got very stressed. We had concluded that we'd only have one family at a time for dinner in the future. It was too tiring to keep everyone on an even keel. It would be a long ten days…everyone went to bed. We headed for the silence of the spa…

Sleep didn't come easily. We had to share our bed with a granddaughter and our one month old grandson slept in a playpen beside the bed. Both kids were very restless and I ended up going downstairs to the couch. During the night my grandson woke up several times for feeding and changing. 'Grandpa' had always been a light sleeper when our kids were young. I couldn't sleep listening to their rustling about. Nothing had changed in this regard.

When I awoke it was way too early. I lay there thinking about Jack. Not long now…Later in the afternoon I'd check my email again. The 'visitors' would go shopping. Then I'd have some quiet time. I'd find time to write more.

I wanted to respond to my wife's journal writings of the previous night. (I had encouraged her in putting down in words what she was feeling). She had written about the weekend away from the hospital when we went to the theatre in Toronto. She'd mentioned my lack of manners towards her. I couldn't remember doing that intentionally but I knew I was preoccupied that evening while waiting for the news of the HIV test results. I'd really wanted and needed to be intimate back at the hotel, but that was out of the question without a condom, something we'd never used ever. I had promised the psychiatrist. NO sex. I had to get out of the hospital no matter what I had to do to please him. I hated not telling her the truth; after all I'd written her a letter in the hospital. It was the doctor who recommended against it. If only I'd ignored them? If only...

Her journal entry was well done that night. I'd told her she had to express more feelings in her writings. This created a place where we could have some dialogue. More than likely that was the only place in the next ten days we'd dialogue about the issue, with our family present 24/7. I needed a nap.

I headed off to the library to check email...alone. I had two messages, one from Jack, and one from my counselor advising me of our next meeting.

Jack's email was just in response to my search of the Church website. I replied, letting him know my itinerary for the next few days. I was going to Disney World next week, but be back on the Tuesday. I'd try to call, wanting to hear his voice again. There were no messages from any of the other guys I'd emailed, but it was too soon or they might not be interested in maintaining any friendships. Time...

Before I logged off I sent mail to Chris' mailbox. I told him about my last conversation with Michael, about how much I'd always miss him, about being with him in the hospital, even though he didn't see me, about my only regret in life...never having actually met him face to face and held him in my arms.

I came home from the library before heading to the supermarket for tonight's dinner. I had barely walked in when my oldest daughter announced that my youngest son-in-law had just lost his job. Just what I needed to hear...it sent me into a funk, as bad news always did. I was upset as I drove off to the store. I quickly shopped and went home.

On the way I kept repeating out loud, "This isn't my problem. It has nothing to do with me. There's nothing I can do to change this. Everyone will manage."...as if saying it made any difference.

And then as instructed in my recent reading, "I am a gay man. I am not going to change. I am good. I have worth." I needed these words to become my mantra. It was a lousy day! Too many stressors...My wife could tell right away. I was that obvious for the rest of the evening...

I was such a bastard yesterday and I knew it. As I sat in the spa the next morning I regretted my actions. Not that I had been verbally abusive. I just didn't feel like communicating with anyone. I was tired and the children, young and old had gotten on my nerves. It had been a long time since I'd been with a baby, especially a crying one. I'd try to make today a better day. It was!

I went to the hot tub first while my youngest daughter made breakfast for everyone. What a treat! I didn't have to cook. After I took my oldest granddaughter to the pool. While the mothers shopped I took all three little girls to a local burger joint where we had lunch and saw live alligators. The girls were very well behaved. When we returned to the condo no one else was there, so I got the girls into their swimsuits and we all went swimming. They loved it! When their mothers returned we stayed in the water another forty-five minutes. After dinner my wife and oldest granddaughter went to the spa before heading to bed.

If there was any downside to the day it was that my wife and I had little time together until we went to bed. Last night she'd slept downstairs with the baby, giving his mother a much needed rest. It was just like my wife. I missed our time together. I would spend the next two days in Orlando at Disney World...more time apart.

After breakfast I headed for the café again. There was a message from Jack which I replied to. I decided to email my 'unemployed' son-in-law back home. I wanted him to know I was there for him/them, especially since he had lost his job yesterday. I tried to impress on him what a great son-in-law I thought he was, and that if he ever needed anything, including money, he had only to ask. I had a lot of respect for him. I needed him to know I was there for him. I hoped my words were supportive.

What can be said? I thought it was a five or six hour trip to Orlando. It turned into eight when I took a wrong turn. The hotel ended up further out than I thought. It wasn't great, but adequate and clean. It was almost eight o'clock when we went out to eat, then it was back to the hotel, TV and bed. Tomorrow would be a long day at Disney World for all of us. Thankfully we were staying over the next night to avoid driving at dark.

When I finally shut off the TV I couldn't fall asleep right away. I lay there thinking about my wife and family. I couldn't predict the future, but hoped for the best with everyone when I finally came out to the girls and their families.

I hadn't been able to check my email before I left, so I didn't know if Jack or anyone had responded. I'd told Jack that we would talk Monday night. I missed the contact. Time to listen to Josh Groban. I did and fell asleep.

The next morning we awoke early, got ready and headed to the park. My granddaughter was excited, yet nervous about some of the rides. We got there just as Disney opened, parked and quickly boarded the monorail. On arrival at Main Street it was decision time. Where to start? For the next ten hours it was rides, food and shows with lots of visible Disney characters. My granddaughter took it all in...seeing it for the first time in her life with me!

From time to time I caught myself thinking about whether I'd ever have the opportunity to bring my other grandchildren there. In two weeks, the secret would be out. Upon returning the whole family would come for dinner. What would be their reaction? I'd have one more session with my counselor before telling them. I'd be seeing Jack—maybe he could offer some advice on dealing with your children. I'd read the hows of coming out in the book I'd been reading. I'd rehearse it and expect a positive scenario.

As the time at Disney came to an end, more wondering. We stopped for the nightly fireworks show over Cinderella's Castle. The theme was "Wishes". As the announcer began he commented about wishing on a star and having the courage to follow your heart and dreams. My eyes glazed over. I was momentarily overwhelmed. I needed a lot of courage if I was going to be true to myself after all these years. As for wishing, so far I'd had no luck! Chris hadn't passed yet, despite being in hospital so long. I'd wished that each night under the stars in the spa. I'd wished for God to take me on several occasions. Wishes didn't cut it. Courage was what I really needed and I'd have to find that within myself…somewhere soon…

After the long ride back to the condo I headed for the café for the latest from Jack. He had a busy week ahead before heading for Chicago. I told him I'd email once more before he left and then would see him when we both got back to Canada the second week of March 2004.

With eight hours on the road I had lots of time to think about our current status. Jack truly was a good friend. He wanted to make sure I was happy. What would happen beyond the next few weeks was still in doubt. Jack hadn't been able to commit to the weekend away yet. So much depended on what happened in Chicago…whether he left his current job and when. Neither was ready to commit to anything more than what we had at the moment. Once we were back in the same city things would take their natural course.

Dear Andrew,

As I write this you are but six weeks old—much too young to understand what I am about to tell you. I am doing this now to explain what you no doubt will be told by your parents—your grandfather was a gay man.

I didn't start out that way as far as I know. Somewhere, probably as an early teenager I had feelings for other young men. I didn't have many male friends in high school, mostly female. One of those was your grandmother. She was essentially my one and only girlfriend. Friends we were—very good friends. We did a lot of things together and thoroughly enjoyed each other's company. I wasn't

really a romantic person and had a hard time showing affection or love, something I hadn't seen as a child either.

Nevertheless your grandmother and I were married and had two children. Our lives together and as a family were very good.

Unknown to your grandmother I harbored basic feelings for men throughout our marriage. Try as I might I was unable to dismiss or erase these feelings.

The evolution of the Internet made it possible to explore my feelings without 'outing' myself to my family or friends. Eventually I couldn't keep these feelings to myself. I acted on these feelings, which ultimately led to your grandmother's finding out my secret.

In the ensuing months I confronted myself through counseling until I was able to come out to my daughters, your mother and aunt. From the moment I told them I was freed from the torturous secret. I was blown away by their emotional support at the time!

Being gay was not a conscious choice. I fully believe one is predestined towards being gay. It is not hereditary or communicable. There is nothing you need to be afraid of.

It did not affect how I felt about your grandmother, your mother, your aunt, you, your sister or your cousins. Every one of them was loved by me to the best of my capabilities. In spite of her shock and disappointment your grandmother stood beside me through what must have been a troublesome time.

Know that I loved you very much. If there is one truth for me to teach you it is to be true to yourself from when you are old enough to know what you want. Don't live your life the way anyone else wants, but you. Live your life to the fullest, enjoying every moment. Treasure what comes your way. It can all disappear so fast.

Be proud of who you are—always…I know I will be proud of you.

All my love

Papa

On Wednesday the girls went to the bookstore and I went to the computer at the library to email Jack. I wanted to email him one last time before he got busy preparing for his trip. Jack had spoken to the minister about bringing a friend sometime. Although he was busy he asked me to call that night so we could talk again.

I acknowledged Jack's comments and wrote a fairly long reply about telling my daughters that I was gay. I went over what I planned to tell them and how, asking Jack's input since he had a similar experience when his children were younger.

I told Jack why I had especially missed him after the day at Disney with all the men walking around and not one to talk to. Finally, I offered my words of encouragement for Jack's interview in Chicago. Jack was a kind and caring person. His interviewer would see that too. It shouldn't matter that he was gay, nor was it any of their business! I would have offered Jack prayers, but I was not in a position spiritually to do so just yet. My prayers didn't work anyways.

I sent off a quick note to my ex brother-in-law in Canada telling him how things were going—that my wife and I had talked more in Florida than ever before. We were looking forward to returning home and getting on with our lives, together and possibly alone. There would be no divorce. We were taking things slowly for now.

Before I closed I asked him to handle the business matters I had been working on for his company. I felt I had done way more than I had thought I could, but it was time for my brother-in-law to find someone else to continue the process. He had too much time and money invested to leave such matters to an unqualified individual. I hoped he'd understand. With that I left the computer and headed back to the condo.

I talked with Jack later that evening. He was not feeling well, possibly the stress leading up to the interview. I tried to assure him he would be fine. Tomorrow I would see what Jack had to say about my coming out plans. I hadn't realized that Jack's kids were in their twenties when he came out. Maybe it wouldn't be that different for me after all.

I'd been thinking all day about the following idea. My wife and I should sit down with pen and paper and write where we wanted to be (i) in two weeks (ii) in two months and (iii) in six months. It would be interesting for us to compare our goals and expectations. It would also give us a discussion point. I'd encourage her to do so as soon as possible. For tonight she was too busy giving our grandson his last feeding before we all went to bed. Only three more sleeps in Florida—which was the way we always explained to our grandkids such holidays as Valentine's, Easter, Halloween or Christmas…

I'd start on my projection list before heading to bed and finish it tomorrow.

In two weeks—

1. *Both daughters and their families would know the truth;*

2. *My mother would be told.*
3. *I'd try going back to Church.*
4. *I'd talk to my counselor frankly about Jack and my relationship.*
5. *I'd attempt to go out at night with 'friends' and not feel guilty.*

Within two months—

1. *My wife and I would review our finances with an advisor.*
2. *I'd spend a weekend away with or without Jack.*
3. *One or both of us would make an initial contact with a lawyer.*
4. *I'd continue to explore other meaningful relationships in the eventuality Jack and I didn't evolve into anything more.*
5. *We'd explore cashing in our RSP's to pay off loans and buy a second car.*

Within six months—

1. *We'd get our finances in order.*
2. *I'd try to get out on a regular basis if just to socialize with other gay men.*
3. *I'd out myself to one other friend or family member.*

The next day started as usual—spa, paper and breakfast. I headed to the library to check my email again, one from Jack, one from my ex brother-in-law. The latter told me to get home, stop the silliness about getting someone else to handle the business matters. We'd talk soon enough.

Jack responded to my ideas about telling my daughters. He advised me to keep it simple; don't tell more than necessary. Be positive and don't get upset with their questions; directly answer things they needed to know. As to how, his suggested statements—

1. *I have brought you together to share something with you, something that sent me to the hospital in October and to counseling since then.*
2. *This is something your mother and I have been discussing for the last three months and I need to get it out.*
3. *After thirty-seven years of marriage, and with the love, understanding and support of my best friend, your mother, I need you to know that I am and always have been a gay man.*

4. *We love you all and need your support even more than ever.*

I thanked Jack for the guidance and again wished him well on his imminent trip. We'd talk by phone on the Friday before he left.

This was a good day. I took my oldest daughter out for sushi at a new Japanese restaurant and came back to the condo for more sun. Later that evening, while the girls fended for themselves, my wife and I went out for dinner…alone.

Dinner was at a new fish restaurant that had recently opened. While the food and atmosphere were excellent, it was our conversation over dinner that was remarkable as we talked about the future, how I would tell the girls and some of her gnawing concerns. I told her how I felt about our decision not to have sex—I no longer was willing to abstain, as long as I was healthy and we did so safely. Since we both enjoyed it we'd continue on. We were even able to laugh at such things as who would get the computer if we separated. We left the restaurant, grabbed a coffee at Starbucks and headed back to the condo…two nights left.

Same morning routine as usual…then a little shopping. At the condo we began packing things up. This was part of the annual trip which I hated. It usually meant back to routine in Canada. This year I was anxious.

Home would be anything but routine this year. While I was headed back to work, nothing else was really predictable. I'd have a long first week—the counselor, Jack's return, telling my mother and then the girls. I would survive it all—I was a much stronger person than when I left, less fragile emotionally. My future lie ahead. I wasn't as worried about that. My wife and I had discussions; Jack and I had discussions before he left on his trip and when Jack returned and we were face to face I'd be in a better position to know how I really felt about him…just a friend? Mr. Right Now? Mr. Right? I had no preconceived idea of how it would go…

What a difference twenty-four hours would make…

Things went downhill at dinner the last evening the girls were in Florida. We took the girls and their children out to dinner at a chain restaurant. We purposely went early so the kids wouldn't be too tired. It wasn't dining; it was eating. The kids were somewhat restless. Their mothers were getting stressed about the long trip home. We ate and left in separate cars with us heading home and the girls doing some last minute shopping.

When we got back to the condo, my brother-in-law and his wife dropped in to say goodbye to the girls and pick up any remaining food as was the usual routine. The girls eventually arrived. The children were rambunctious as the girls tried to pack the van. My oldest granddaughter had a disagreement with her aunt and dissolved into tears. I felt my anxiety level rise; I began to sweat and headed outside for some much needed fresh air. Just let them be gone...all of them, including myself.

I disappeared briefly to call Jack, wishing him a safe and successful trip and went back to the crowd. Finally packed, the in-laws took their groceries, bade farewell and the girls and their kids got ready for bed. I headed for the spa...alone.

My wife never understood my passion for music. She used to tease me about my tastes for 'mellow'—Streisand, Yanni, John Tesh, Marc Anthony and more recently Josh Groban. (I once paid two hundred US dollars to see Streisand in concert—for one ticket).

Music spoke to my soul. Even if I didn't understand the language (Andrea Bocelli) I felt the music in my heart...

As a child this had always been the case. One of the first solos I ever performed was from the Broadway play, "Carousel". It was entitled, **"You'll Never Walk Alone"**.

> **When you walk through a storm**
> **Hold your head up high**
> **And don't be afraid of the dark**
> **At the end of the storm is a golden sky**
> **And the sweet silver song of a lark.**
> **Walk on through the wind**
> **Walk on through the rain**
> **Though your dreams be tossed and blown**
> **And you'll never walk alone**
> **You'll never walk alone.**

At the moment, that moment, I felt alone. I felt all of the progress I had made in the last six weeks might be fleeting. Gay men are not necessarily always happy, no more or less than straight men or women for that matter. What did I expect? No one ever told me that my journey would be easy...joy was still so elusive...

I stayed up after everyone had gone to bed to write again. I wrote honestly about the day. When I finished I was off to bed.

Morning came early...around six-thirty everyone was up and getting ready to go. By seven-thirty the girls were headed back north. My wife and I headed for a quick time in the spa, got dressed and went out for a quiet breakfast. After that she went shopping with her sister, while I went to check my email. Two emails from Jack before *he left. Short and to the point. I'd see him Thursday night. I emailed back, not knowing whether Jack would be able to reply from Chicago. In less than twenty-four hours we'd be headed back north as well. Ahead…the best and the worst week of my life. By next weekend my children would know that I was gay. This part of the journey would finally be over. My life as a gay man would begin without any fear or anxiety of my family finding out accidentally. Would the truth set me free? No matter how the children reacted there was no turning back now…*

That evening we had a surprise birthday party for my sister-in-law, turning sixty. Her husband had organized the party, inviting all of their northern friends and some Florida friends—about fifty people. I had organized all the food for the party; my brother-in-law handled the beverages and bills. I was pleased, when as usual, the food turned out to be terrific. I excelled at such things, whether it was dinner at home for family or friends or special events like our annual appetizer party where everyone took turns preparing a dish. I was pleased with myself…must be a gay characteristic? The party ended and we cleaned up and headed back to the condo and one last visit to the spa, under a full moon. Was I grasping for signs I was on the right track? Probably…

Bright and early the next morning we'd be heading north for the two day trip home…

HOMEWARD BOUND

*We left the condo at six forty-five to head north. I drove first while my wife read. After two hours we stopped for breakfast. She then drove while I read her book. In fact the book had been given by us to our youngest daughter for her recent thirtieth birthday. It was Mitch Albom's "**Five People You Meet on the Way to Heaven**".*

It wasn't a lengthy book, but my daughter had thoroughly enjoyed it. It was an easy read. The synopsis is that an eighty-two year old circus worker dies suddenly at an amusement park. (Coincidentally, my mother's father was a circus worker when he died). As he heads for heaven he meets five people who in some way he touched during his life. I was reading it fairly well until I came to the chapter where the old man met his father with whom he had a challenging relationship. Sound familiar? It stopped me cold. It was too close to my own situation with my father. I quickly closed the book not wanting to read the details. I sat there thinking about what it would be like to meet my own father. The image brought tears. I thought I had dealt with this issue when I wrote the initial letter to my father while I was in the hospital and through the subsequent counseling and last letter. Obviously the issue was still there. I couldn't hide the tears from my wife as she drove through the Alabama countryside.

I tried to compose myself. Finally I was ready to read again. I was okay with it now. The moment had passed. I finished the book and took my turn at the wheel. The rest of the trip was unadventuresome. I did know something was bothering my wife. She was unusually quiet. Obviously my earlier tears had upset her or made her begin to worry about what life back home would be like after these six weeks away. At this point she didn't know the reason for the tears. I'd have to explain later.

Nine hours later we stopped at a motel south of Louisville, checked in, went for dinner and returned to watch TV. Each of us turned to our journals and began writing...

When I read her journal I was somewhat surprised. She was angry about me deciding to leave Florida early. I hadn't thought much about it. My counselor asked me to change my appointment and I really thought nothing of it. I should have consulted her. Hindsight didn't solve the problem. As to her feeling upset at the thought of never *going back to this place…I thought we agreed a new place would be found; this place wasn't warm enough, or any longer 'fresh'. We'd find somewhere else—Mexico, South Florida, Arizona…who knew?*

What she was really concerned about was whether 'we' would be able to do this next year, fearing we might not be a 'we' one year from now. I'd told her that nothing was predictable. I couldn't make any promises right now. As she herself said, "One day at a time".

In her journal she also expressed concerns about my physical safety…abuse from a stranger. I never met anyone directly but always asked them to meet me at a coffee shop before becoming involved. I didn't hesitate to walk away if I didn't feel comfortable and had done so.

Regarding my health and disease issues, I had made myself very aware of the signs and symptoms of possible diseases. I made visual assessments of my 'partners'. Since the hospital I'd had regular HIV tests and gotten hepatitis vaccinations as a preventative measure. In truth there was no positive assurance from abuse and/or disease but I was as careful as I knew how to be. I protected her as best I could by now using condoms when we had intercourse. There wasn't really much more I could do to reassure her, other than to abstain from all relations with other men. That wasn't going to happen now. She knew I was gay; it went with the territory. I didn't mean to be flippant about it—that was just how it was.

ONCE MORE INTO THE FRAY

We got up early and headed out on the second leg of our trip home. It was an uneventful drive—good weather. Once home we began the task of unpacking the car, putting things away and sorting out six weeks of mail.

That done, I checked my email—nothing from Jack in Chicago (I didn't expect any) and two from my youngest son-in-law finally responding to mine from Florida. He'd found a new job already. I should have known he would. He seemed content with the new place, with basically the same salary.

After a quick dinner out at the hamburger joint we came home. I checked email one last time. Marco was online and we chatted briefly. My friend would check his schedule and see if we couldn't meet some time during the week. We'd met a couple of times before and enjoyed each other's company. It would be good to see him again. It would also be the first time I had gone out with my wife knowing that I was meeting someone. I couldn't help but wonder how she would react. We'd talked about the eventuality of this. Talk was one thing; the reality was another.

The next day we were back to the routines of our lives, well almost. I got up, dressed and headed out on my 'paper route'. The term was coined to explain my coffee and newspaper routine at the nearby coffee shop. I shopped for groceries, got a haircut and then headed for my counseling appointment. Much of this time was taken bringing the counselor up-to-date on the last six weeks. When I told the counselor about the letter to my grandson I had to stop twice as my emotions overwhelmed me. I was finally able to continue. We talked about it for awhile. I admitted that one of my greatest fears was not being able to see my grandchildren after telling their parents the truth. Time would tell.

After dinner I got an email from Marco. He'd be home from work by eight o'clock. Could we get together as planned at his house? I was truly looking forward to seeing him again after all this time.

When I got there he was still dressed in his business suit. We opened a bottle of wine and sat on the couch watching regular TV. While we watched and drank we began talking. It was just like the other times. We talked about his work, his family and friends. He seemed so comfortable sharing personal details of his life with me. Strangely, he had been admitted to Teachers' College but passed it up because he already had a great fulltime job with good benefits. He had one sister and a brother. He was the baby of the family and had led a very straight Italian life. He'd never been married, (except to his job) but had dated women. We really enjoyed each other's company and before we realized it was three hours later. He had to get to work early the next day. We said our goodbyes, gave each other a big hug and I headed out the door and home.

When I got home my wife was still awake. She inquired as to how the evening went and I said it had been very nice. I hoped we'd do it again soon. She seemed alright with my going. I was glad she understood, even though it must have been on her mind all night—where was I? With whom? What were we doing? I knew that I couldn't do what she was doing without a lot of resentment. My peer counseling group could never understand my situation and my wife's acceptance of my coming out.

I went to bed and fell fast asleep with my arm on my wife…until, as usual I got too warm, rolled over and hugged my pillow, listening to no music. I felt contentment.

The next morning we were taking care of our middle granddaughter as her mother was working. She was never a problem and amused herself well. I was looking forward to my group counseling session that evening. With the exception of the salesrep, none had ever been married. I realized none of them would have any additional input about coming out to children, but I enjoyed the circle of friendship—gay men talking about gay issues, which confronted us all. Unfortunately the 'flamer' was on vacation and I wouldn't have the opportunity to work on my homophobia which I had experienced towards him in the first two sessions. I had already expressed my feelings to the counselor. I'd work on it when the man returned to the group.

Counseling went well. I updated the guys on what had occurred while I was in Florida. There were only three of us—the salesrep (J), the architect (R), and myself. R had finally told his European mother. J expressed concerns about his current partner. Once again it was good being there. It was comfortable. We left with our customary hugs and went on our own ways…

The next afternoon I decided to phone my ex brother-in-law. He was going to be visiting my daughter that night. I wanted him to know I had not yet told the children and to please not mention it. I wasn't going to be there myself as Jack was coming home and we planned to meet. I was taken aback when he warned me against telling the children. He felt it wasn't necessary. I could continue seeing men; there was no reason why the children should know. I let him know that wasn't an option. My brother-in-law was frustrated by my adamant position. The conversation ended abruptly with my brother-in-law's voice sounding disappointment in my decision not to go back after all these months.

The man I thought had accepted me for what I was—a gay man—was suddenly sounding like this was a temporary condition which could be corrected...

No one can ever understand what I'd been through all my life...the feelings, the urges, the desires for men. I didn't remember them pre-adolescence. From adolescence on they were always there. I hid behind the mask of normalcy—job, marriage and kids. I was firmly closeted to all who knew me. Cyber sex and chat lines made it possible for me to open the long closed doors to my soul. The rest was up to me!

Jack arrived home and we finally got together later that evening for the first time in six weeks. I'd gone to Jack's with lots of anxieties and expectations. After our time together I would finally know if Jack was Mr. Right Now...

The evening started with a two hour long talk. Jack was back from his interview in Chicago and really excited about the possibilities of going back to school. While we were talking Jack received two phone calls from friends wanting to know how things had gone. I began to read the book Jack had brought me—**"Finding Yourself in Transition"**. Jack had thought I might enjoy it. As I read it I was realizing that what the author was writing, I was living. It wasn't a gay book as such. It was a book written about people going through many of life's transitions—divorce, death of a loved one, unemployment, etc. The writer wrote of endings, voids and new beginnings. He was in my head. Every word he spoke, spoke to me. For the first time, I came to realize it wasn't all about being gay; it was about being myself, physically, psychologically and spiritually. The ending had started; I was facing the void. There was a lot more road to travel...

We talked more after Jack got off the phone. Each agreed that what I needed was time alone. I didn't need Jack to go off with me for a weekend. I needed to get away by myself...reflection and discovery...maybe affirmation...

What followed was the usual man to man routine. I felt comfortable, but different. I didn't know, but was fairly certain this was a friendship with 'fringe benefits'. It was not a new beginning! Jack was meant to be part of my transition. Chris had initiated my ending. Where I would be after Saturday night would indeed be the void—shedding my last important mask so that I would become more of whom I really was after all these years. Would I like who I really was?

I had started the journal months back in an attempt to find out who I was. At the time my gayness was not something I could bring out. Now that I was out I had thought it would be the end of the journey and hence the title of my book...I was now too realistic to believe that. It was an ending indeed, as Robert Brumet wrote in the aforementioned book. I was still facing a long journey to the new beginning. I finished the book and passed it along to my wife.

Tomorrow was the day I had long dreaded. My children would know that their father was a gay man...Sleep wasn't easy, not that I worried about tomorrow. I woke at seven thirty feeling good. There was a lot to be done before dinner. My wife went out to lunch with our best friend. I stayed home to finish up a couple of things. When she hadn't arrived home I decided to take a walk—something I hadn't done since my stay in the hospital.

Experiencing some sense of coming full circle I put on Marc Anthony's CD **"Mended"** and set out for my walk. I had listened to this same CD hundreds of times during my online relationship with Chris. Perhaps I needed closure...I wanted to play it one more time. It wasn't an emotional time now. The one thing I decided that it was time for my wife to listen to this one song—the song that had said so much to me.

As she listened she became emotional. Why hadn't I said something sooner? Why did I let myself become so desperate back in October? I hugged her tightly, trying to explain what the song really said to me. The song was **"I Wanna Be Free"**.

In one hour the children would arrive for dinner...

THE AFTERMATH

It was ten thirty. The house was quiet. After dinner, as planned, I sat them down with my wife beside me and told them what I had planned to say. Surprisingly I wasn't emotional. I told them honestly and without my voice wavering. All the time, I was watching their faces for reactions. My youngest daughter tensed up almost immediately. After I was done she got up and left the house. I didn't run after her as I had done on many occasions when she was growing up. Those demon teen years! This wasn't something I needed to fix or could fix. She needed time and I would give her as much as she needed...

My older daughter took it unexpectedly well. While she was surprised she didn't become emotional as I had thought she would. She came over and gave me a big hug. I was also surprised by her husband's reaction—seeming acceptance. This was probably the one person I had been truly worried about. In fact, during dinner he had made a comment about not wanting anyone gay around his son. When he said that it almost made me change plans about telling, but I couldn't go back now. I was pumped. It had to happen tonight!

After everyone else had left my younger son-in-law stayed behind. He had been curiously silent after the announcement. No doubt he really didn't know what to say. It must have been quite a surprise to him. He was a lot like me—usually a quiet type of guy—probably why I felt so close to him.

In an attempt to open some discussion I asked him if I could still go on the planned golf outing to Michigan to which he nodded approval. The three of us sat there having a drink as if nothing had changed two hours earlier. Meanwhile we all wondered where my younger daughter might have gone.

He eventually headed home. It was time to talk to Jack. I'd said I would call him after I made the announcement. It was getting late. I decided to send him an email, inviting him to phone if he was still awake. Otherwise, I'd see him in the morning at Church—the first time I was attending.

I remained calm after all of this. If my daughter had a problem it was hers. I wasn't going to accept ownership of it. She needed time indeed. Just before eleven *o'clock my son-in-law called to tell me she was home with her family. I wouldn't try to speak to her tonight. Let her be with it as my counselor would say.*

And so here I was almost five months after being hospitalized as suicidal—out to my wife and children. I could never have imagined surviving the telling back then. I'd totally underestimated the degree of love, support and understanding of my wife. She was an exceptional person.

Tonight felt like the end of my journey. Ahead lay the void. Just as life to this point had been totally unpredictable, so would the months ahead. I'd begun a new journey of discovery—not to find out what I was, but who I was and what I wanted to do with the rest of my life.

The sun would come up tomorrow. I felt the worst was over and behind me...

THE SPIRITUAL JOURNEY BEGINS

Well…no sun…just more snow! I really hated winter. We got up and went for coffee and to read the newspaper. After that I was going to Church. I hadn't been there except for weddings and baptisms since I was a child. I had no real expectations, other than to see whether it had any real meaning to me during this void. Jack had invited me out to lunch after the service. My wife was going out for a debriefing with her girlfriend, much as I was doing with Jack. I wouldn't be gone all that long; just in case my younger daughter needed to talk…I was hopeful.

The Church service was excellent. The whole congregation was welcoming. Jack introduced me to a few people before the service. Each hugged me unconditionally—male and female. They were a varied group, young, old, black and white, etc. This wasn't a gay church. There were couples with young children. The minister reminded me of a favourite aunt. She stood in the middle of the congregation and chatted about life—almost like a talk show host. There were two soloists and a keyboard player. The songs were non-traditional, unhymnlike with various beats. Everyone joined in. It was a warm feeling. I knew I wanted to come back next week. Afterwards we all met for coffee and light snacks before going our separate ways. This was special. I hadn't been in so long. I wished my wife could experience this. Jack and I headed for lunch where we talked about my experience, both in the Church and last night with my daughters.

When I arrived home my wife was upset. She'd talked to our oldest daughter. She relayed the message that her sister was very angry about last night. I didn't want to hear this second hand, but would let her tell me herself when she was ready. She hadn't replied to my email—I didn't think she would—being the adult I tried phoning her making the first move. There was no answer; she was ignoring the phone or out for the afternoon. Probably the former. I tried to be positive. After all these years in dealing with my children I finally came to realize some things were beyond my control…

Over the next few days, emails flew back and forth, first my older daughter, my younger son-in-law, my youngest daughter (still angry but not without trying to understand). My older son-in-law sent my wife a nice supportive letter. It was my younger son-in-law's letter that meant so much to me. He didn't really understand why I was gay. He wanted me to know he loved me like a father and that he'd always be there for me. He invited me out for a few beers and talking. This was the special person I knew he was.

"People take different roads seeking fulfillment and happiness. Just because they're not on your road, doesn't mean they've gotten lost."

Those words jumped off the computer screen in an email from my younger daughter. It had been almost a week since I'd come out to her. After four days of passing emails, I'd finally talked to her on the telephone. It was brief, but I'd heard her voice. I was still giving her space. That same evening she'd gone to see my wife at work. Healing was a slow process for everyone. I knew that all too well by now.

I was back at work now. Things were very tense between my work mate and me. His wife had the baby—a boy. He was born two weeks premature and had some breathing problems. I didn't press for details. We talked a little more later on—work related only. I wanted to talk more. I knew I still needed him as a friend...but he needed lots of space right now with his own concerns.

At my next counseling session I was really pumped again. I was out. My youngest was coming around. I was okay with that. I wanted to move forward and explore the gay world. For the first time I told the counselor my doubts about Jack. I was beginning to think he was truly Mr. Right Now. I was always the one to initiate our conversations and meetings. I was the one trying so hard to please him. I'd gone to his Church to try to understand him better. It was all about doing whatever for him. In our times together and in his emails he never expressed any emotional thoughts about me. Jack was supportive. He provided an ear and a shoulder. The bottom line was, besides the sexual gratification, we had nothing in common. For one thing, Jack was much more religious and spiritual than I. That part was bothering me as well. I was having serious doubts...but I wasn't ready to go it alone.

Another day at work followed by another group counseling session. The other guys sat mesmerized as I told them about the coming out dinner. I expressed my doubts about Jack. Each chimed in with what was going on in their lives. The guys were quiet and preoccupied. J sat very quietly for the first hour before the counselor got him *to open up…troubles with his partner still. He didn't have much to say. R praised my braveness.*

Before they went their separate ways again the counselor asked if they had any suggestions for my immediate future. I'd said I was going to Toronto for a weekend to explore…alone. The conversations turned humorous as the guys started to give me the dos and don'ts of Toronto's gay scene.

I left the session and headed to pick up my wife at work. Subconsciously I needed to talk…about what…I didn't know. When she was done we headed to a mall bar for a drink and some food and then home. No real conversation. It was St. Patrick's Day…

Had I come this far, made this whole lifelong journey, sacrificed my family's happiness to end up alone?

THE VOID

Thinking back to my recent reading of the book which Jack had given me, the first fifty-seven years of my life had ended. Everything I knew and was was history I thought. I had officially entered the "Void". I began to seriously contemplate my future. The early morning email from my daughter brought me crumbling back to reality. I headed for work, after sending her a short reply, "I am feeling lost!"

I'd told the counselor I didn't need to see him weekly anymore. I was wrong! I'd also told him I knew there'd be a down time to my recent high. I didn't know it would come so soon. I'd make the call before heading to work. I was in the very bottom of a pit and I couldn't see the way out!

After work came a breakthrough. We went out for dinner with my youngest daughter and her children—finally face to face. It really was like old times. As we left the restaurant I hugged her and thanked her for the emails of support. This seemed to be working out…

Later I was back at the computer, checking emails and the gay chat room, looking for friends just to chat. A previous chatter came on with whom I'd never been able to connect in person. We planned a meeting, but before it could happen there had been a family emergency. I wasn't upset. I wished him well and invited him to get back to me when things were settled down for him. No rejection this time…

The weekend was coming up. Maybe I'd meet Jack the next evening after dinner. Strangely, or ironically I knew Jack and I needed to talk more also, just as my wife and I needed to do all of our married lives. I didn't want to push Jack; he was only Mr. Right Now. He needed to know that is how I was feeling so there would be no regrets for either of us.

The evening with Jack went well. I cooked dinner for the both of us while he relaxed. His mind was on his acceptance to the programme in Chicago. After dinner, while drinking a couple of low carb beers, we talked a little about the future and how I'd miss him. The evening ended with the usual routines; we gave each other hugs and I headed home. How many more of these evenings we would enjoy together would be known soon.

Church on Sunday was a good experience again. The atmosphere was one of love and support. Jack was still basking in his trip to Chicago. Some of his peers in the States had word of acceptance. He hadn't found out yet. Early in the week he'd know for sure, most likely accepted. After Church I headed home; he headed home to do some work.

After dinner that evening I was to meet a new friend for coffee. I was anxious. This was the same person who had to cancel due to the family emergency—Alan. We chatted many times in the past. We met and talked and talked until it was two hours and many coffees later. We agreed to meet again without the coffee. Early to work tomorrow.

At work I received my annual monetary review. It went well. Not only did I get a raise, but also received two certificates for sales achievements. It was a great day. Later we went for a coffee with my wife's girlfriend.

I slept well, but for some reason I awoke in a funk. Sitting at the computer working on my novel I received an email from Jack, who was at work. I let him know I was feeling funky. When he pressed as to why, my response was basically that I was feeling scared. I reaffirmed it had nothing to do about him moving away. That was totally true.

I was still meeting new guys as I had done Sunday night. I was learning what I was looking for in a friend. I was becoming aware of the character traits I didn't like and the type of person I wanted to avoid.

Mid-afternoon I chatted with a person in Toronto to whom I'd been speaking for a while now. He explained to me what he had experienced—being anxious to find Mr. Right. If only I relaxed and enjoyed the moments someone would come along. Reduce the verbiage and desire to meet someone again. Let them make the move if that's what they wanted. Mr. Right would make himself known in time. Explore and discover what it meant to be gay...

The funk began to lift. I was making progress after all, but I wanted to move too fast. This wasn't a race. For the rest of my life I would have to face the highs and lows of being a gay man with human emotions...Come to think of it so does a straight guy...guess I am really normal after all...at least in emotional terms.

FINI? Not quite...

That night I had a dream. In the dream I was walking down my great grandparent's old street. They had both been dead for over twenty years. It was changed. The church across the street was gone. A new subdivision was in its place. My grandparents came walking out of their house wearing very fashionable off-white suits. They looked like they were in their early fifties. My grandmother had on a long skirt slit up the side and high heels—very unlike her earthly dress. She gave me a hug and said I had changed. I cried. My grandfather gave me a great big bear hug and said to me, "You're not in Chicago anymore" and we just held each other. As I awoke I heard Canada geese flying overhead—a sign of winter's end.

They've been watching over me! They know I've changed and it doesn't matter. I don't need to rely on Jack (Chicago). My emotional winter was over! I'm in the springtime of my life again…which just happens to be my favourite season.

I had decided after the revelation from my great grandparents to end this story. I was out and felt I had their blessing and support. Last week at group counseling was very unsatisfactory—the young guys seem to be in such a different place than I. For this reason I have decided to see my counselor for more one on one sessions next week. After that I'll see what I need. I get the impression my wife doesn't think this is necessary. I am in transition. Some days are really good; some are dismal. I despair of the future—together with my wife and possibly alone, and I do mean alone.

Since stopping my journaling my wife and I hadn't really discussed the situation much. She was going out with our best friend to the theater Sunday night. I had plans to meet someone, possibly.

I had been with Marco once since returning and with Jack a few times. The evening with him was so nice, lots of conversation, etc. until he fell asleep!!! Oh well…I guess he certainly was relaxed…

Jack had been very supportive—even when I had been bitchy. He was headed to Mexico for ten days with his old 'partner'. Actually he lives there. At the end of June he heads for Chicago for two years. After that he will definitely be relocated elsewhere. He is Mr. Right Now! I'll move on…but am undecided about the long weekend in Toronto at the end of the month.

I did meet again with my ex brother-in-law who now seems to understand who and what I am and he can accept that.

The gay dinner club was okay, but it seemed like a lot of the guys were partnered. I did meet two guys who seemed nice and exchanged email addresses, but they too were partnered. I felt slightly odd being there—a married man.

Last night I had a strange dream. Someone both my wife and I know had invited her out for a late dinner. He did so in front of me and my youngest daughter. After hearing her accept I ran away naked and started to fly with these two large white birds. I guess some type of geese or swans. When I actually woke up I felt momentarily suicidal, but realized this is still NOT an option for me. This flying experience was a reoccurring dream from childhood.

I was supposed to meet someone this evening to whom I previously talked, but it never panned out so I continued to work on my novel...now half entered in text. Hopefully it will be done by the end of the month and I will seriously look for a publisher.

Church tomorrow...I decided I can't be Bryan anymore. I must be the real me. My wife is going to the theater with our girlfriend. I chose not to go. It will be a good opportunity for her to go without me being there. I expect to meet with someone, but who knows what will happen. At this time I am limiting myself to three regular guys, Jack, Marco and the teacher. I have no intention of getting involved with anyone else. They are all nice, safe guys. We mutually respect and enjoy each other.

The women went out. Once again I was alone after all! Jack was packing for his trip. Neither of the teachers was available. The younger one let me know early in the day—family obligations. The other got back to me around ten fifteen. He was tired after a long day. By then it was too late to go out. I worked on my novel—I'm better than halfway there. After last night I've started to write again. I need the outlet...I am just so frustrated these days...

This morning at Church I felt such despair amid the Palm Sunday service. Every song affected my emotions. With Jack gone for ten days I only have my counselor to rely on. I worry that that isn't enough right now.

I had told Jack I probably wouldn't go away to Toronto at the end of the month, but I may have to. I just can't seem to connect with anyone here...part of the reason I need the counselor again. I am terrified at ending up alone! I just don't know what to do...

I woke up at five forty-five on Monday, my next work day. I seemed to be doing that a lot lately. I slept well. I put on my headset and listened to Marc Anthony hoping to fall back to sleep. When I woke up again it was time to go to work. I quickly emailed Jack wishing him a safe trip. I would miss him—we talked or chatted almost daily. He had been like a second counselor since I met him. Ten days with no communication at all would be difficult. Even in Florida we were able to keep in touch. For at least the first five or six days I would be busy—counseling, grocery shopping, late nights at work. Jack's absence and my schedule would give me little social activity time. I hoped I'd at least see the teacher after Easter, before Jack came back home, but that wasn't certain.

After work I received a brief email from a married guy in Michigan I had met at the gay dinner a week earlier. We had talked. He had a partner, younger, but still lived at home with his wife too. I had told him about my situation; he had contacted my counselor to request counseling as well.

Although he wouldn't be able to join our group for another month, he thought we could meet for lunch and just talk. We had lots in common. He'd found the book, **"Outing yourself"**, *which I had recommended and had lots of questions. It was agreed that we'd meet for lunch on Friday, the day after Jack returned from Mexico. At least this would give me someone else to talk to who could appreciate where I'd been before coming out. And just maybe I could help him in his hour of need—nothing more.*

I had a late appointment with my counselor the next day. In the morning I had a coffee with someone I had spoken to a few times on the chat line—coffee—nothing more. He seemed nice enough but not my type of guy.

My counselor and I discussed my obsession with finding someone to hook up with. I knew it was an obsession, but after the events of the previous week I was desperate for male companionship—any male companionship. He offered several suggestions to help me with the problem—first of all limit my computer time to one half hour per day. I promised I would try…guess I better buy a timer! He agreed I should keep writing. I needed the outlet for my feelings. He encouraged me to project myself forward five years to see what I expected life to be like. My wife and I had tried that in Florida. It was enlightening.

For my part I saw myself with a regular guy—someone with whom I could go out for drinks, dinner theater, etc…possibly someone to travel with. He asked if I saw myself cohabiting and I answered in the negative. But who knew? I still saw myself in an open marriage as long as my wife would tolerate my activities and me. He asked me to imagine what I'd do if I had complete freedom now. I had to answer that I had no idea! I had gone from home to marriage, like so many couples in the sixties. I guess I'd never known freedom like today's young men and women who delayed marriage until their early thirties. My older son-in-law was one such person, traveling the world before he settled down in marriage.

I told him about my terror at ultimately being alone. He understood, but said I couldn't obsess about it. Instead I needed to focus on where I wanted to be and then how I could get there. By taking my focus off of the end result I'd be able to explore my options and be more relaxed. We concluded by discussing my upcoming Toronto trip and what my expectations were, but not before I broke down when I mentioned my only regret through all of this—not being able to let Chris know I still cared and never being able to say goodbye. The counselor raised an interesting question. What if Chris wasn't dying, but was simply a young closeted gay man who knew he'd gotten in over his head? Was his death a charade too? I didn't want to hear that right now.

Taking my counselor's advice I sat down and wrote down where I was at the moment, and where I want to be in five years. I think I was honest. It's not so much projection, but more of a gut feeling. He feels that if I know where I want to go I'll be better prepared to take the necessary roads. I think it would be good for my wife to do the same thing. We'll see.

April 7, 2004 Where Am I?

1. *out to wife and children*
2. *successful part-time job that I like mostly*
3. *nice home, good pension, nice car*
4. *in a regular relationship but unfulfilling*
5. *regaining spirituality by attending church*
6. *moderately healthy—HIV—but with high blood pressure*
7. *doing moderately well financially*
8. *obsessive about meeting the right man and spend too much time on computer*
9. *emotionally in turmoil*

April 7, 2009 Where I Want to Be

1. *moderately healthy still*
2. *in a regular, fulfilling relationship with a man*
3. *financially stable*
4. *roof over my head*
5. *totally retired*
6. *enjoying the finer things in life like travel, theater, etc.*
7. *married? Cohabiting?*
8. *still best friends with my wife*

9. *family still want me in their lives*
10. *happy with who I am*

As I finish writing Marc Anthony sings in the background on the restaurant's muzak…time to head to work before tonight's group counseling session. Hopefully it would go better than last week. I felt so detached from the other guys that night, which is why I headed back to the counselor again.

Great night at the counseling session. We covered so much territory with only the three oldest guys there…we were all over the place with our discussions and before we realized it we'd talked almost two hours.

By the time I got home dinner was ready. My wife had made a great new pizza recipe and of course we had wine. After dinner we shared our five year plans—many similarities except for my finding a regular friend to spend time with.

All went well until my wife mentioned that she had a fleeting thought of taking down our wedding picture. It felt like a knife and I immediately became tearful. How could she? Why? Maybe she should burn our photo albums too? It really hurt. I shut down and left the room. My wife did too. When I came back upstairs she'd left the house. Laying in bed I couldn't help but think about the situation. Part of the reason why I wasn't able to move was that I didn't want to move on! It's unbelievable to most people, including her I guess, but I love her more than ever; it's just that I need to be with a man too. If she decides this doesn't work for her then she needs to tell me! I don't want to torture her for the rest of her life…

As for the wedding photos, it was a marriage of best friends and that's for life as far as I am concerned…

So damn disappointing! On Good Friday we went out for breakfast and then worked around the house and garden. It was a beautiful spring day, made more so with the thought that after dinner I was finally going out to meet someone—actually two guys whom I had previously spoken with. We met at the one guy's apartment. After chatting and watching some TV the one guy decided he was tired. He'd just come from his girlfriends and decided now to go home. The apartment's owner had injured his arm in the afternoon and was on pain killers. It was time for me to leave. What a wasted night!

I drove around for a half hour in frustration. The gay bar which I'd never been to was closed. Just when I'd gotten the nerve to go! I went home to the computer and wrote in my journal, after emailing our host for the evening. "Don't call me; I'll call you". Fat chance that would happen again…

Part of the reason I get obsessive is a result of what happened tonight. I hate feeling like this. I get upset when this happens—at least they weren't' no shows' but might as well have been.

Today I have one bruised, but not bloodied ego. I know it shows. My wife asked me what happened last night. I said, "Nothing!" Wasn't that the truth? One more lesson on the road out. Just how long was this road anyways? Would I ever reach a destination? Still too many questions…off to work again. Just imagine how I'd get if I didn't have a job? My wife would certainly agree to that. Right? [She still is reading this, so every once in a while I throw these statements in so she can say "I told you so!"] Yes, dear!

Everyone was here for Easter dinner. As usual it was somewhat chaotic with six adults and four children. Our oldest granddaughter seems to be growing up. She seems a long way from the turbulent young girl she was a few years back. The girls all adore their 'baby boy'. The two younger girls get along most of the time and enjoy playing with each other.

*We had a great dinner which actually started with my oldest son-in-law's famous Thai spring rolls. He ended the meal with his equally famous hot oatmeal cookies with an ice cream filling. Tomorrow we'll start dieting again LOL. I was a little quiet. Several times I went back to our last family dinner, after which I came out. Everything seems back to normal now, but I know it will never be that way again. I've been reading a new book, **"Secret Lives of Married Men"**. I see myself in so many of the men's' stories. Not all ended in divorce—many of the couples stayed together after the husband's initial outing. A few, like me, had been caught in the act.*

I just wish I had a crystal ball. I've mentioned to my wife about seeing a psychic or a fortune teller. Our future is unpredictable, at least by us.

The day ended with me meeting one of the teachers for coffee. We hadn't seen each other for quite some time, actually several months as his schedule was chaotic—he played golf, curled, was involved in minor hockey all winter…Your typical suburban guy. When he wasn't playing, he was working long hours. If he were married I don't know how he'd fit that in. It never ceases to amaze me how many guys my age are out there. No pun intended. He wasn't out at all, likely because he was still teaching and had a few years to go before he could retire.

We enjoyed each other's company and I headed home feeling that, at least for tonight, I wasn't as bruised as the previous night…the ups and downs of gay life…Ironically, it was a bright sunny day the next morning as we headed for work.

I'd never thought about this until right then. How many sunny days does one get in a lifetime? I guess birth should be our first. After that, although we're all too young to realize it—learning to walk and talk. Moving through our school lives has many sunny days which we tend to forget. For guys, a driver's license is a bright sunny day. Graduating from college or university should be bright if one has a job prospect. After that, marriage, the birth of one's children, their successes, their marriage and the birth of their children—your grandchildren should be bright too. (Oops, almost forgot…our first sexual experience should be, but not likely for most people). We all go through life hoping for sunny days. When they occur, in fact or as an event, we all experience highs in our emotions.

On Easter Sunday, the minister had gone on about ridding ourselves of the traditional religious significance of the Resurrection. The truth of the story lies in the message of Jesus. We need to resurrect our spirit. That was His example to us. Sunshine resurrects most people's spirit—factual or eventful.

Why is it human nature to forget the sunny days? Or is it just me? Supposedly sunny events like marriages and childbirth always seem cloudy to me. Remember how this story started? Why do I allow these clouds to roll in on joyous occasions? What is it about me? Shouldn't all family occasions be sunny days? I have so much in life, everything anyone else would be envious of—a great wife, children and grandchildren. Millions of people will never experience that.

I needed to reawaken my spirit—my internal, emotional sunshine, before my life goes dark forever. I know my family finds it strange that I attend Church on Sundays now. I hadn't done that in forty years. As my counseling sessions are healing my mind somewhat, attending Church is a step towards healing my spirit, maybe just a baby step, but eventually I'll be able to walk tall. I hope…

There's an old John Denver song that begins with, **"Sunshine on my shoulder makes me happy"***. I want that sunshine. I need the sunshine. I should open my eyes to the sunshine around me; maybe I'll find it in me then. Nobody can find it for me.*

As I was driving to work, I started to think, "Do you realize how many popular songs have the theme of sunshine?" Think about it. I counted at least thirteen. Interesting number, eh?

After work I headed home. It was nice to have a short work shift.

We had Easter dinner leftovers; my wife went out to get some cold medicine. Tomorrow I had lots to do. My brother-in-law and his wife were coming for dinner on their way back from Florida. Wednesday would be work again, with counseling; on Thursday I worked late. On Friday I was supposed to have lunch with the fellow from Michigan. Just lunch! I had turned down a guy who had earlier asked me to go out.

I could see it would be a long, quiet evening. My wife wasn't feeling very energetic as a result of her cold. I checked my email around eight o'clock and there was a message from the man who had the family emergency three weeks earlier. How about tonight? On the spur of the moment I agreed. He was single, with his own place; he was a nice guy. During the evening my friend encouraged me to stay overnight. I couldn't do that yet. Not now, but not never. In time, it could be, but this was way too soon. I headed home, did some writing and headed to bed. I quickly fell asleep with thoughts of a really pleasant evening. Tomorrow I'd be making train and hotel reservations for my trip to Toronto. I'd also learn the results of my most recent HIV test...

Tests negative; reservations positive. Next weekend I'd be heading to Toronto for three days. Three days of what I didn't know. Maybe sitting alone in my hotel room. I'd talked a couple of times to two guys there who seemed normal, but gay. The only commitment so far was to meet for coffee, as was my usual scenario. I wanted to explore the gay scene away from this city. I expected it would be less awkward and more invisible. Even if the guys and I didn't hit it off, I'd at least have someone to show me around. I expected I'd be uneasy. Utmost in my mind was security and safety. I wasn't prepared to go wild—it wasn't my nature...or so I thought.

We had a nice visit with my brother-in-law and his wife. After dinner we visited my older daughter and her family, before returning home to drink more wine before heading to bed. Laying there my mind went back to one of the conversations I'd had with a man in Toronto. He was mid-thirties and a professional. He was hoping to meet an older man for a long term relationship. Although he had not been successful, he was not interested in a married man. Just what my wife said would happen! Guys wanting a regular relationship wouldn't consider me. As a married man, I didn't want to resort to playing the field. How could I ever win? I wanted more than a physical relationship. Was that too much to ask at my age?

My wife and I were working way too much right now. We hadn't been spending much time together. We often worked different shifts. When we were alone for a few hours was when one of my friends would want to get together. I could stay home, but I needed and wanted to get out. Every day I was becoming more of the problem in our marriage. My wants, my needs, my desires…Why should she be content with being a second priority? Then again, in her journal, I came third after the kids and herself. Our friendship seemed to be suffering. After the weekend in Toronto we seriously needed to see a marriage counselor before we ended up hating each other. I didn't want that. Over time she would come to resent my meetings. How could she not? I had started this journey seeking joy in my life. I still hadn't really found it; I had now compounded the situation by taking away any joy she might have had in our relationship. She never said that to me. That was my perception. It gnawed at my soul…

Counseling went well again—just three of us, as J was out of town. The guys talked about what I could expect in Toronto and where to go safely. I appreciated their concern. M was very quiet again—seemed to want to be somewhere else. He had a very big assignment due at college. R was pretty laid back too. He was still going to bars in Detroit, but wasn't seeing anyone right now. We talked about the games that some gay guys play and the whole issue of honesty between men. It really wasn't any different with straight guys and the women in their lives. At eight thirty we all left until next week.

Friday was a very interesting day. The only planned thing was lunch with the fellow from Michigan. We had a great first meeting at a nice restaurant. Unfortunately he was partnered and I respect that. This relationship will be strictly friendship and that's okay. After lunch I went home, did some ironing and sat outside for a while. Hard to believe it was spring and temperatures soared into the seventies. When I went inside I checked the computer, quickly sending a note to the Michigan guy thanking him for the nice lunch. Checking the chat room there was a new person I hadn't spoken to before—Sean. Looking at his picture and profile prompted me to email him. Online we talked about likes and dislikes. Don't know if this was an omen or not, but he too was partnered eight years. Why are these guys here anyways? They had an open relationship so he invited me to meet him. Apprehensively I agreed. I didn't want to be a third party.

He was exactly like his picture—not tall, but good looking, slightly balding and had a great personality. He was a nice guy, with a nice apartment he shared. Our time together was equally nice. I certainly would like to meet him again, and he agreed. Maybe we would or maybe we wouldn't. I guess it depends on what fate has in store…

Speaking of fate, after picking up my wife at work, and going out for a late dinner I went online again. This time I checked the Toronto room to see if any of the guys I'd previously talked with were there. They weren't, but I did start to chat with a mid forties widower who worked for the government. He'd been widowed for five years, non partnered and seeing no one regularly…or so he said. We chatted for a good forty-five minutes…it was after midnight. He was about forty-five minutes from downtown Toronto, but agreed to meet me for coffee and show me around. If this worked out as planned I wouldn't be exploring alone. That would make me feel better—a little less vulnerable in the gay area. We ended our conversation trying to speak French…his was as good as mine. Tomorrow was work. On Sunday I'd meet Jack at Church, seeing him for the first time in almost two weeks…interesting week ahead…

Counseling again on Tuesday, followed by another gay dinner club get together. On Wednesday group counseling. Work Thursday and Toronto on Friday morning. Not much time to see Jack…maybe not a bad thing. As the time for him to leave grew closer, we needed to move further apart…there was no future for us and I think we both knew that now. I owed him a lot, but not the rest of my life!

After work on Saturday my wife picked me up and we went home. I started to get dinner ready, but she went to bed, sleeping for the next twelve hours. Her health was worrying me. She's rarely ill and doesn't miss work. After waiting for two hours I made dinner for just myself. I keyed in more pages of my novel. Bored, I headed to the chat lines looking for the new guy—Sean—I met on Friday. Not there, nor anyone else I knew. I entered the Toronto room again and start chatting with a forty-plus guy nicked Marauder! We have a good chat about attitudes of gay men on chat lines. He's not unlike me. When the conversation ended I returned to the usual room—no Sean. I begin to chat with another fifty-ish guy and agree to meet for a quick coffee. Less than forty-five minutes later I am home. He was someone to talk to. Not my type. Feeling lonesome I turn on the TV and watch Paul Newman being interviewed by Heather McCartney. Why can't I find a Paul Newman? LOL

STARTING TO UNLOCK THE THIRD DOOR

Sunday I met Jack at Church. Sick wife went to work…what can I say? I'm feeling/sensing some awkwardness and don't sit with Jack. My imagination at work? I don't think so. The sermon was interesting. The minister told a story about three people, each knocking on the door of a castle, where there is a party going on. The party represents life. The first person goes to the door, hears noises and walks away; the second knocks timidly, gets no answer and walks away; the third knocks boldly, gets no answer and walks in where he is warmly greeted by the other guests.

Her message always speaks to me. I am that timid knocker still, waiting for the door to be opened in my life. True, I did open one—coming out. I wanted to open the next one in Toronto next weekend. I still was not sure I wanted to join the party. If I opened the door, would I forever close another? A light bulb moment…were these the doors to my closet? I guess I thought there'd be only one door. How many doors were there ahead?

We chatted after Church about his recent trip to Mexico to see his old partner. He tells me to call as I leave to visit my oldest daughter. Only her husband and my grandson are home. I take my grandson for a walk so his Dad can cut the grass. When he falls asleep I take him home. While he sleeps his father and I have a serious discussion about his father and about me. It felt good being able to talk with him openly. We talked about my going away for the weekend. Up to this point only my wife knew why I was going or that I was going. He seems to understand where I am coming from.

I picked up my wife early from work and she went to a clinic. It was a severe sinus infection and she would stay home from work the next day. Once again she went straight to bed. I went straight to the computer…hoping to find someone to spend some time with tonight. Jack checked in and we had this silly cat and mouse game of chatting. He was tired after driving five hours in the morning to get to Church for the Sunday service. I was getting tired of listening to him talk about Mexico and his upcoming move. This door was ready to close. I told him I was going out alone for a *coffee and would talk later. I told my wife the same thing. As I drove off I felt truly alone. I sat in the coffee shop parking lot thinking and decided I'd call Jack and invite myself over. He approved. That was a mistake…more Mexico and Chicago. I finished my coffee and left forty-five minutes later.*

At home, my wife was still sleeping. Guess what I did? This time I met another seemingly nice guy from Toronto—fifty-eight, divorced when he told his wife he was gay, children, looking for some nice quiet time, just looking for a friend. He also worked for the government. Were all the guys in government gay? He gave me his home phone number and his work number and we tentatively agreed to meet on Friday. It might be a game. I'd find out when I called him…

On Monday I wrote Jack a long letter—my Dear John letter. I thanked him for all he'd done for me, his patience, understanding and wise counsel. Now was the time to move on. I wished him well and said goodbye, but I didn't send it just yet. Soon.

Dear Jack;

This is the letter you knew I'd ultimately write. The time is right. I must follow the dream of my grandparents, not in Chicago if you remember.

You have been a good and trusted friend these last several months. You were with me through my various emotional highs and lows. You were a friend, with 'fringe benefits' as you so aptly described it. You never led me to believe it was more than that. You were honest. I came to fully realize that last night when we had coffee I needed to move on.

You want more and so do I, but not with each other, we're on two different roads which happened to intersect briefly. That was God's plan. As I told you before He sent you to me when I needed Him most. You reconnected me to Him. As you prepare to open your next door so must I. You taught me not to see rejection as a bad thing, but to consider it personal growth. I have grown, but there's a lot more growth to accomplish.

Whatever happens from here on, I will always be indebted to you for your friendship, guidance, patience and understanding. You need to focus on the future with no distractions right now. You cannot be my lifeline. That has to be God's role. I have to let God, as I have learned these last few months.

I wish you all the abundance you so richly deserve and all the joys your chosen path will elicit. God has chosen you for all the right

reasons. I know He is with us both no matter what happens in the future.

Goodbye my best and most trusted friend!

With this it was truly time to move on, physically and emotionally. It had only been a matter of time.

Tuesday I had a dental appointment, then a late afternoon counseling session, followed by the dinner club.

TAKING MY LEAVE?

Counseling was somewhat disturbing. We talked about me going through the door—coming out to my wife, the second door—coming out to my children. We eventually came to the third door. All of this came about from the Sunday Church service. My third door, I finally admitted was leaving our home. My wife and I no longer seemed to enjoy each other's company. It was more than her being ill recently. We got in each other's way. My failure to get things done was truly a problem. I finally finished our income taxes after two weeks of pestering by her. I still was spending too much time on the computer which she resented. She threatened to cancel our Internet service! Right now we didn't seem to like each other a lot of the time. I wasn't helping I know. I felt things might get better if I just left, but I was afraid to open the third door. Working so much didn't help us right now.

My father opened the door and never came back to his children. He never had a civil conversation with my mother after that. I broke down as I imagined my walking out that same door, having it slam shut behind me. I didn't want history repeating itself. I didn't dislike my wife. I didn't want to have the door slam. I still needed my kids and my wife. I still loved them.

The counselor listened intently. Maybe I needed to look further ahead. IF the marriage ended what kind of relationship/friendship could we have? We were each other's best friend, as I constantly stated. I guess I wanted us to be the friends we'd started out to be. Looking back to those first years we were great friends. We had fun together. I was attentive, buying flowers and little gifts often. We went out with friends and had good times. There was no sex then, at least not before marriage. They say you can never go back, but that's what I wanted to do—go back to our early years, when we actually liked each other ninety-five percent of the time. Let's be real here...

Maybe something good would come from living apart for a while, although it would be difficult for our family and our finances. We could still be involved with each other, our kids and our grandchildren. We could still see our mutual friends. We could actually date each other. This time there'd be no masks on my part and no false expectations. We could even occasionally have sex! After all, I'm not one hundred percent gay! I'd still help out with maintaining the house. The car would be a problem. We could still travel together and with our close friend.

Opening this door wouldn't necessarily be a bad thing. It didn't have to be like my parents—full of hate and spite years after the marriage legally ended. I didn't even want a divorce and saw no need for a legal separation unless she wanted it. We could live apart indefinitely (sometimes I'd sleep over if she wanted).

This could be a positive move…we needed to sit down and talk about it. I would try to do it before I left for Toronto. We needed to peek through the door and imagine what the other side might be like…
Was I trying to have it both ways? Maybe. But just maybe that would and could be the best solution for both of us…
After counseling Wednesday night we'd talk…on the other side of the coin, she might not want any part of this arrangement…

When I got home my wife was sitting quietly pretending to watch TV. She'd read the journal entry and had been quite upset. She wasn't sure she wanted to go out for dinner as planned. I insisted. Funny we always talked better when we were out…and we did. I tried to explain what I had said. Leaving was not imminent, nor was it a fact. It was an option, granted an option I thought we should exercise. In my mind, I thought three months from now would give us time to explore the realities. We talked quietly and I attempted to honestly answer her questions. She was as scared as I was; I think we both agreed to try the dating thing, trying to rekindle the friendship. This time she would know the real me, not the masked man she'd married almost thirty-eight years ago.

We peeked through the third door and just maybe we could live with what we saw in the immediate future.…going through it would be painful for us and our children when we told them; it needn't slam shut as it had with my father.
I was leaving for Toronto tomorrow with no firm expectations of what I would do or whom I would see. I knew I wasn't searching for Mr. Right and I didn't think I was still searching for the real me.
My journey was by no means over, but I was now feeling confident that I wasn't and probably wouldn't follow in my father's footsteps…

CULTURAL AWAKENING

On Friday, April 23, 2004 I went to Toronto. There I hooked up with one of the three guys I was supposed to meet. It wasn't at all like I had been anticipating. The others were no shows and didn't return my phone calls. After our brief encounter I ventured out into the gay village. It was momentarily exhilarating, walking openly for the first time among gay men. For the next forty-eight hours I explored the bars, male strip clubs, coffee shops and the well-known spa.

Each time I left the place unfulfilled. I looked around at the men there. I didn't see me in their faces, mannerisms or actions (in public).

On Saturday evening I stayed at the strip club until closing, walking unnoticed down Yonge Street at two a.m. briefly grabbing a hot dog from a street vendor. I was still hungry physiologically and emotionally.

On Sunday I awoke late and checked out of the hotel. I headed to a place in Yorkville for breakfast. As I sat down on the third floor eating, I literally looked down on my life as the rain fell steadily. Something was missing from the picture I saw. I walked through the Village, heading for a local mall. It was soon time to board the train for the long ride home.

I was momentarily back in Florida on that bus to Biloxi. Where was I really going?

When I saw the middle-aged couple in front of me snuggling and enjoying each other's company I knew what I was missing—my wife!

I had come to this point in my life, resolved that I had been missing something all these years. For the last six months I had expended all my energy affirming that I was gay—gay chat lines, gay dinner club. Gay group counseling and homosexual encounters.

I hadn't found what I was looking for. The gay scene was still surreal to me. Did I really belong there?

The closer I got to home the more I questioned myself. Why wasn't what I had enough?—Good, loving wife and family. My wife accommodated my sexual explorations. Amazingly!! Was what was occurring part of a mid-life crises?

As I got off the train I wanted to believe I would work through this—no more chat lines, no more counseling, no more encounters, get over Chris. I was prepared to stop my transgressions. I didn't...

ONE MONTH LATER

I found myself kneeling at my father's grave—devastated…alone…on a rainy Friday morning in May. I swept the grass from the stone marker, which no longer bore a picture of his face. How ironic! I started to cry again…

During the last month I continued to chat, continued counseling and continued the encounters, although not as often. Jack and I continued to meet, but strangely we only had drinks and talked. He had gone to Mexico to visit his former partner. After that our friendship was more platonic. For the most part, I met with another young man frequently—Alan—in the county—usually once a week at night. We enjoyed each other's company despite our age difference. In some ways he was a younger version of me, except he was able to explore his sexuality at an age I couldn't. Each encounter became more involved. Each departure left me wanting more of his company. My mind worked overtime as usual. I decided to visit my doctor and request an STD test…my old paranoia running rampant.

Mid-May, late in the evening (or early in the morning, considering it was one o'clock in the morning) I logged on to the chat room and was invited by two men to join them for fun, I didn't hesitate, even though my wife was asleep and I should have been as well. We played around for about an hour and I headed home to bed. What had I come to? What was I thinking? I'd promised to play safely. I was perilously close to moving beyond that.

I didn't see Alan for a while after that. We met briefly in the chat room, but he seemed to be avoiding me. Perhaps, Like Chris (according to my counselor) he realized he had gone too far as well. I began to chat with another young man in a city near Toronto. It was déjà vu—young, single, curious, late night IM that went on for some time, almost every night. I was open; he understood.

Recognizing a recurring pattern, I realized I had to stop searching for young men; after all I was nearly fifty-nine years old. I needed company of men closer to my age. None of the young men were Chris. They never would be. I vowed to make no more additional contacts beyond those I was already involved with…Well at least I'd try.

What I needed to do was to become socially involved in the gay community. This couldn't happen in my city, so I looked to a neighbouring city—Detroit. There were regular activities for gay men in my age bracket and situation.

Towards the end of May I went away on a golfing weekend with my younger son-in-law and his friends—just as we had done in October before I entered the hospital. It felt good, even though I was guarded. On the second night I downed a forty ounce bottle of vodka and passed out on the bed. When I awoke it was eight-twenty in the morning. I was alone. My son-in-law was gone. My last memory was playing cards. How did I get here? What had I done? I had no memory beyond the card table about one o'clock in the morning. I panicked thinking I might have revealed something or done something in my stupor. When my son-in-law appeared he assured me that I'd just fallen asleep. I was relieved. Golf was great!

On the way home to Canada I had two hours to think. I had to change my ways. I had to find a meaningful way of letting Chris go.

Mid-week, after counseling I arranged a symbolic release, inviting Jack to come with me for support. I purchased two red helium balloons, representing Chris and myself. Standing in the park with Jack I attached my only picture of Chris and a small card. After meditating with Jack for a few minutes, I composed myself and read my tearful goodbye speech.

Letting go of the strings the red balloons climbed quickly into the night sky headed for the same stars I'd prayed under in Florida. When they were out of sight, I hugged Jack and we left the park. I headed home. Finally he was gone! I could once again try to move on...

Unfortunately the very next evening sitting at the computer I received a long-awaited chat invitation from Chris' friend, Michael in North Carolina. He'd just come from visiting Chris in the hospital in Minnesota. Chris was going to be released from the hospital sometime in July!

I was not sure how to respond. I was happy for Chris, and for Michael. I had just let Chris go less than twenty-four hours earlier. I queried Michael about his condition. Unable to use his legs, he was in a wheelchair and had some slight mental impairment, which I didn't want interpreted. He was recovering from the cancer...

I was afraid to seem too excited. I had told Michael about the ceremonial release. He questioned my response to the great news. Had I given up on Chris recovering? It had been six months now. Michael had told me to let Chris go back in November. He himself had been very angry at Chris for putting him through this charade of his death. I was frustrated, as was Michael. How did he expect me to take this great news? I had no idea IF Chris would remember me with his disability or IF he wanted to ever contact me. I didn't want to get my expectations up for a reunion in the future.

Getting nowhere with Michael, we said our goodbyes for the night. How could he question my affection for Chris after all these months of waiting? The tears poured *forth again. Why God? Why now…the very same questions I had asked back in November when I thought he had died…Your timing was pretty shitty God!*

The next day I found myself at the cemetery asking my father the same questions. I needed answers. They were in me. Jack told me that. My counselor told me that. The minister had told me that in one of her sermons. I wanted to rip them out of my body!

When would the merry-go-round stop? It had to stop. I wanted off…My heart couldn't go through this again with Chris. But, what if he still needed me? What if he didn't need or want me? That was the real question and only he could answer those…six weeks from now.

I left the cemetery and headed for a quickly arranged counseling session where I poured over all of the thoughts running through my mind. I let loose all my emotions…. It felt good…

Later that evening I attended a social function at the Church. It was a night of Broadway music and chocolate. We all had baked something as a fund raiser. Unfortunately, several of the songs got me thinking again. I left as soon as it was over.

Sean had invited me over to his new place for awhile so I went. It helped to take my mind off me. We had some fun. Afterwards I went home and chatted until two o'clock in the morning when I finally went to bed. I worked two in the afternoon until eleven at night, so there was no socializing.

When I awoke on Sunday I headed for my 'paper route'. My horoscope read as follows—

You have fallen and more than once in your recent struggle with uncertainty and upheaval, but you have not been disqualified. You have not conceded defeat, nor should you. Your indomitable strength will yet win the day.

On Sunday I got up and started to cut the lawn. While I was doing that I suddenly realized why Chris had come back into my life, although not quite yet. My readings about radical forgiveness had shown me that people coming into your life are there for a reason. I knew why he had come into my life earlier—to help me with my father and sexuality. I had an epiphany—he was coming back so I could finally say the goodbye I hadn't been able to do in November! Then I could truly move on…it felt good knowing that. I had an answer at last! It did come from within.

The sermon at Church was once again meant for me! The song lyrics spoke to me as well—

Let God the past; tomorrow can wait; the time is now!

The balloons literally burst Sunday evening! That came in the form of an email from Michael about Chris. Along with the information about Chris' actual condition, came the word that Chris had asked about me. He still remembered me through all of this!

The next twenty-four hours were dismal. I pondered Chris. He needed me now more than ever. Would he want me? Should I go there? Maybe it was still me who needed him. What if it wasn't reciprocal?

It was once again Jack who brought me down to earth with only three questions—

1. Have you ever met him?
2. Do you REALLY know him?
3. Do you really want to be his caregiver for the rest of your life?

The answers were No No and Yes respectively, or so I thought then.

I needed answers NOW…I went out to the coffee shop for a coffee and to think. As I gazed out the window, I read a bumper sticker—

Jesus died for you so he wouldn't have to live without you.

How prophetic! Was this an answer? I knew it not to be so…

The following day I spoke online to the fellow from near Toronto—Tigger. He urged me to contact the hospital where Chris was and talk to him. I did have an idea where he might be. Cautiously I called on my cell phone. **No one by that name here!**

I couldn't play this game anymore. Thanks Tigger for pushing me! Enough was enough. I emailed Michael and asked for Chris' hospital address so I could send a card. I knew I'd probably get no reply. Now really was the time to say goodbye. Before the goodbye I had to forgive and be thankful. Whoever he was, whatever his motives, he had brought me this far, and that was a whole lot further than I had been when we first started chatting last summer.

REVELATIONS AT LAST

After the episode with Michael I went a little crazy. Chris needed me. He was paralyzed! I wanted him. I despaired. When I told my wife what was happening she said I should go to him if that's what I wanted and would make me happy. Take my savings and go to North Carolina…at what cost?

Between Jack, Tigger, Mark and my wife I was down for the count as they say in the WWF. I had two distinct choices—stay or go.

Falling back on my newly acquired spiritual awakening the answer was clear. Chris' Spirit would look after him. He had his family and friends there. He really didn't need me. The reality was this was a May-December infatuation! I had to get real. I emailed Chris telling him how I felt. I wasn't sure he would see it since he was still in the hospital, but I sent it anyways. I would always be a friend; there was nothing more I could be…

I was continuing to meet with Alan. There was no attachment there; we enjoyed the time we spent together. We were mutually satisfied with the status quo—no strings…at least that's what we both agreed. He was younger than me as well, but it didn't seem to matter when we were together, which by now had been many times.

At Church on Sunday we had a guest speaker from Missouri. He spoke about the second and third comings. I was hesitant at first as I wasn't sure I was ready for theological talk. What intrigued me was when he talked about spiritual awakening. I felt I was experiencing that finally.

The second coming, unlike traditional interpretations, was not about Jesus, but about individuals being spiritually awakened. That fit. As he continued to speak about how this would occur, I began to take notes. In my portfolio was a copy of the lyrics to a song by Marc Anthony, "I Wanna Be Free" that I had listened to constantly before and after entering the hospital. I'd always thought it spoke to me about leaving my family and exploring the gay world—the other side.

At that precise moment, as I re-read the lyrics, I had the first of three revelations that morning.

These words were not about freedom and coming out of the closet. They were about my finding my Spirit and listening to it—my personal spiritual awakening. I was *stunned at the significance now. My journey was destined to be spiritual as well as moral.*

The second revelation came as the speaker talked about something called "Delectable wound"—a temporary state of euphoria from which we never want to be released. That explained not wanting to let Chris go, even after the balloon ceremony. I thrived on being wounded.

The third revelation was with regard to Spirit. Was it possible that Chris was the human incarnation my own Spirit? Had my Spirit been transformed into Chris' body—his words questioning me, encouraging me, pushing me out of the closet, sending me to Jack and eventually towards my awakening? I couldn't be sure, but it all made sense at this point. I'd have to talk with the Minister about that one.

I was overwhelmed. I had answers!

At Church on Sunday, the same speaker delivered a sermon about love. One quote struck me—

Love is bold, daring and radical.
Expect the unexpected.

The 'fourth' revelation—that explained my wife's continued support and accommodation. She really did love me. How could I have not understood that? What else explained her commitment?

When I got home I wrote the quote on our memo board for her to see. Underneath I wrote, "That's you." And then I wrote, "I do love you too!"

I was more 'out' today then at any time in the last eight months. I was out of the closet and was beginning my journey to true spiritual awakening and understanding. Going back to my earlier reading, **"Finding Yourself in Transition"** *I had made the transition and was finally coming out of the 'void' of the last two months. The new beginning was in reach.*

EPILOGUE

So where was I?

I was out to my wife, children and their families. Four friends knew—my wife's girlfriend, my ex-brother-in-law and his wife, and my reluctant work buddy. Obviously the guys in counseling and those I met knew, although some knew me by another name I used in the chat room. Jack knew the whole truth! He had been my confidant all these months. My doctor knew; I had no choice there.

I was fairly at peace with my father, Chris and Michael. Radical forgiveness had taught me the value of their individual gifts to me. Through attending Church I acquired a Spirit who continued to support and guide me.

I had found a couple of friends who supported me—Ron—who was also gay and married. We met for lunch and commiserated. At the moment, Tigger (Shawn) whom I met on the chat line was there to kick my butt when I needed it.

Alan was my only regular 'friend' right now. We tried to get together at least once a week at his place. We were honest about our relationship—it wouldn't be long term. For now, for each of us, in the parlance of the chat rooms…that was **kewl**…

0-595-33786-4

Printed in the United States
25101LVS00004B/177